NEW JACK CINEMA

Hollywood's African American Filmmakers

STEVEN D. KENDALL

J. L. DENSER, INC. MARYLAND

ALL INQUIRIES AND CORRESPONDENCE
SHOULD BE ADDRESSED TO:

J. L. DENSER, INC., 14528 CUTSTONE WAY,
SILVER SPRING, MD 20905
(301) 236-5330

LIBRARY OF CONGRESS CATALOG CARD NUMBER:
92-075983

ISBN 0-9629513-1-5
MANUFACTURED IN THE UNITED STATES OF AMERICA

THIS BOOK IS DEDICATED TO **MOM**, **GRANDMA** AND TO MY LOVELY WIFE **JUDITH** FOR HER CONTINUED SUPPORT OVER THE YEARS. SHE HAS TAKEN A LEAP OF FAITH WITH ME MORE TIMES THAN I CAN REMEMBER. LAST, BUT CERTAINLY NOT LEAST, TO MY WONDERFUL SON, **CHRISTOPHER**, WHO AS AN INFANT, PREPARED ME FOR WORK ON THIS BOOK THROUGH HIS RIGOROUS, SLEEP DEPRIVATION TRAINING PROGRAM.

IN MEMORY OF **KATHI SPIVEY**, WHOSE ENDURING FAITH AND SPIRITUALITY LIVES ON AS AN INSPIRATION TO HER FAMILY AND FRIENDS.

Preface

What is a "New Jack"? That may have been your first question upon picking up this book if you were not familiar with the slang term. One of the earliest uses of the phrase has been linked to journalist Barry Michael Cooper.

During the 1980s Cooper wrote several magazine articles that singled out music producer Teddy Riley as being the founder of "New Jack Swing," a type of pop music influenced by urban street culture. Riley's unique music, wrote Cooper, was a mixture of computerized sounds composed of elements from funk, gospel, hip-hop, and jazz. The street culture content of New Jack Swing, argued Cooper, was expressed by the craving many inner-city youths had for the expensive cars, clothes, and jewelry made possible via the drug trade.

One of Cooper's articles, about a highly organized gang, made its way to musician/producer Quincy Jones. Impressed with Cooper's knowledge and coverage of the street scene, Jones provided him with the opportunity to revamp a screenplay which later became the basis for the urban crime drama, *New Jack City*.

In time, the phrase New Jack became part of the cultural lingo in the early 1990s, as evidenced in an article by rappers Big-D and Doctor Dre, in their slang dictionary written for *Emerge Magazine* (March 1990), "Hip-Hop for the Unhip." The authors defined a New Jack as, "A member of the African American cultural vanguard of hip-hop music."

A few years later, author and host of the music video program, *Yo! MTV Raps,* Fab Five Freddie, referred to a New Jack as, "a person new to a situation making an attempt at being the best," in his book, *Fresh Fly Favor: Words and Phrases of the Hip-Hop Generation* (Long Meadow Press, 1992).

My definition of a New Jack, as applied to African American film directors, is a blend of the two discussed above. I would consider the filmmakers featured in this book to be members of the "African-American cultural vanguard," and many of them are "new to a situation (filmmaking) making an attempt at being the best." They not only attempted to be the best, but had to in order to survive the Hollywood system, as they were not often afforded the same access and opportunities as their white counterparts.

I chose to use the phrase "New Jack" not only because I thought it would make for a catchy title, but also because the slang term aptly described, I would argue, the passion and commitment with which a new generation of filmmakers brought to their work.

Given my definition of a New Jack, I have excluded directors like Richard Pryor, Prince and Eddie Murphy as each had the opportunity to direct, in my opinion, as a result of their previous success as actors. Each of these men, at the time they directed their first films, were extremely popular performers whose access to the director's chair was dictated by their superstar status, which disqualifies them from discussion in this book.

I have also made it a point to include only those films which received national distribution in the U.S. and are thus available on home video for additional study by the reader. There are also a number of excellent independent films which merit discussion, but unless they received wide exposure, I have declined to include them here, as the focus of this work is on New Jack films which have reached a mass audience.

The films selected for discussion are arranged in the approximate order of their theatrical release, but the text is organized in such a way that the reader can ignore the chronology and read about a particular film or filmmaker by simply consulting the table of contents.

The book is organized into three parts:

Part One: The Beginning of the New Jack Era, covers the years 1986 to 1990 when at least four filmmakers, Spike Lee, Robert Townsend and the Hudlin Brothers, stood out and set the tone for those to follow.

Part Two: The Renaissance Year, examines 1991, the historic year in which there were more feature films directed by African-American filmmakers, and released on a national basis, than in the entire previous decade.

Part Three: The New Jack Spirit Continues, looks at the period after the Renaissance Year as established New Jacks secured a foothold in Hollywood while up and coming African American filmmakers made impressive debuts.

Each chapter consists of a short biographical profile of a specific New Jack director and background information regarding their work. Box office figures for specific movies are from *Variety* magazine unless otherwise noted.

In the Appendix, the reader will find a short list of production credits, for each of the major films discussed.

I do not consider this book by any means to be the definitive, final discussion of African American filmmakers. It should be looked upon as an introduction of sorts.

To be quite frank, I wanted to write this book, in part, out of a desire to maintain a dialogue about the new generation of African American filmmakers succeeding on a national scale.

It is my hope that this book will reach the hands of young readers as I wrote it primarily with them in mind, thus the easy-to-read style and the affordable price.

I developed an early interest in filmmaking by devouring all of the books on the subject in my local library. In light of my personal history with books, may this book find its way into schools and libraries so that students of all ages may hopefully experience the same educational catalyst I encountered through reading.

Steve Kendall
Arlington, VA
July, 1994

Acknowledgements

A special thank you to the following folks:

My colleagues at The American University. Specifically, Sandy, John, Glenn and Ann, thank you for your confidence in me and your support over the years.

All of my students, past and present, thanks for your energy, enthusiasm, inspiration and for keeping me on my toes.

Megan Snyder and Anju Wadhwa, my graduate assistants who read the manuscript and offered insightful, extremely helpful reviews.

My editor, Dennis Wong, a man who never complained when I missed every single deadline. Thanks for the creative freedom you afforded me in the writing of this book, and your patience, which at times rivaled that of Job.

Jane Jeffries who did initial layout and design for this book.

Maria Yap and her talented team at Option X, the firm that was responsible for additional layout, design, and production, thanks for your talent, wisdom, and above all, your extreme patience and understanding.

Kenny Simms, a photojournalist from KDKA TV in Pittsburgh, PA, who first inspired me to pursue a career in film and television.

Patti Fears for the inside info, and for providing tasty Thanksgiving grub for my family each year.

"... we also rejoice in our sufferings,

because we know that suffering produces perseverance;

perseverance, character; and character, hope."

Romans 5:3

NEW JACK CINEMA

Hollywood's African American Filmmakers

CONTENTS

PART ONE:
The Beginning of the New Jack Era (1986-1990)

I

She's Gotta Have It

Spike Lee: Writer/Producer/Director/Actor/Editor

(Island Pictures, 1986)

THE BLACK FILM CATALYST

If one were to isolate the catalyst responsible for the current resurgence of films made by African Americans, the search would likely lead to director Spike Lee. His highly successful directorial debut film, *She's Gotta Have It* (1986), demonstrated to many white Hollywood executives that a black man, directing a film for and about black people could be accepted by a mass audience. Moreover, Lee served as a role model for a new generation of would-be filmmakers waiting in the wings.

HOW HE GOT THE NAME "SPIKE"

Spike Lee was born on March 20, 1957 as Shelton Jackson Lee in Atlanta, Georgia. His nickname, "Spike," was given to him as an infant by his mother Jacquelyn Shelton Lee. Reportedly, she named him Spike because he was a tough baby. Shortly after Spike was born, his father jazz bassist Bill Lee, in search of a better climate for jazz artists, moved the family first to Chicago, Illinois then to Brooklyn, New York. Due to Bill Lee's refusal to change with the times and play electric bass, work as a musician became scarce for him. This prompted his wife Jacquelyn to help support the family of five (Spike, the eldest child, has a sister and three brothers) by acquiring a job as a school teacher in Brooklyn. Jacquelyn Lee never got the chance to see her son become a great filmmaker as she died in 1976 of cancer while Spike was a student at Morehouse College in Atlanta, Georgia.

THIRD GENERATION "MOREHOUSE MAN"

Going to college was practically a given for Spike as his mother was an educator and both his grandfather and father attended Morehouse College, thus making him a third-generation "Morehouse Man." As a Mass Communications major he took classes in journalism, radio, and television. He worked on campus as both a radio station disc jockey and as a reporter for the school newspaper. Toward the end of his years at Morehouse, Spike made several Super-8mm films and developed an interest in filmmaking. It was also at Morehouse where Lee made a number of friends who would later work with him, specifically, schoolmate Monty Ross.

ALMOST KICKED OUT OF FILM SCHOOL

In the fall of 1979 Lee entered a three year graduate school program at New York University (NYU) to study filmmaking. He came close to being dropped from the film program during his probationary first year. Professors routinely evaluated student work to determine who would continue graduate studies at the school. Spike's first-year short film, called *The Answer* (1980), caused him a bit of trouble. The ten minute film told the story of a black filmmaker who is given the chance to make a multi-million dollar remake of the 1915 racist film, *The Birth of a Nation,* directed by early film pioneer, D.W. Griffith. Some of the faculty accused Spike of not knowing proper film "grammar" or structure. Spike believes that his professors were upset because his film was not kind to Griffith, the so-called "father of cinema."

SPIKE MEETS DICKERSON AT NYU

Despite the reservations of some of his teachers, Lee was invited back for a second year at NYU with a teaching assistantship. The assistantship allowed him to work in the school's film equipment room while receiving free tuition. This in turn permitted Lee to use the tuition money provided by his grandmother to fund his student films.

During his second year at NYU Lee began to work with another black film student, Ernest Dickerson. Dickerson served as camera person for Spike's second-year film *Sarah* (1981), a portrait of a black family celebrating Thanksgiving. The duo followed that with Spike's master's thesis film, the hour-long *Joe's Bed-Stuy Barbershop: We Cut Heads* (1982), about a small-time betting operation run out of a barbershop. The film was a launching pad of sorts for both Lee and Dickerson. Dickerson's cinematography was noticed by others, which eventually led to professional work. As for Lee, he won a student academy award for *Joe's*. The film was screened for the public as part of a New Directors/New Films festival at the Museum of Modern

Art in New York and went on to be shown at a number of other film festivals around the country and on public television.

As a result of the attention garnered by his thesis film, Lee received representation by two talent agencies, William Morris and International Creative Management (ICM). However, he soon found that both agencies were unable to secure work for him in the film industry. This prompted Lee to depend on himself to make it as a filmmaker. After graduating from NYU in 1982 with a master's degree in filmmaking, he earned money by cleaning movies for First Run Features, a small New York based distribution company (co-owned by Lee's friend Barry Alexander Brown who would later edit *School Daze, Do The Right Thing,* and *Malcolm X).* While working at First Run, Lee wrote a script for a feature film that he wanted to direct.

THE SPIKE LEE FILM THAT WAS NEVER MADE

By the summer of 1984 Lee was set to direct a film called *Messenger,* from his original screenplay about a bike messenger who becomes the head of the household after his mother dies. The film was to star actor Kadeem Hardison. Unfortunately, things quickly unraveled for Lee. The Screen Actors Guild (SAG) interrupted the start of production because they would not allow him to use non-union actors in the film. SAG considered the project to be a commercial venture which required union performers. Lee wanted to use non-union actors because the expense of union wages would be too great for his low-budget production.

His film was dealt a death blow when its producer, who was a longtime family friend, failed to raise the necessary funding. As a result, Lee had no choice but to call a halt to his project just days before production was about to begin.

AFTER *MESSENGER* LEE BOUNCES BACK

After the demise of *Messenger,* Spike Lee quickly went to work on a story called *She's Gotta Have It.* It was about a young back woman and the three men vying for her affections. Lee's intent was to create a film that would be inexpensive to shoot, yet highly commercial. Interviews with his female friends served as the research for the lead character "Nola Darling," a sexually free woman who is unwilling to settle for just one partner.

Production began on the film in July of 1985. Lee's college friend Monty Ross drove up from Atlanta to serve as production supervisor on the film. They started shooting with less than $20,000, largely from grant money that had been designated for the defunct *Messenger.* To raise additional money Ross worked the phones every day soliciting donations from their friends.

Several locations in New York City, within close proximity of each other, were chosen as Lee had neither the budget, nor the time, to do otherwise. The filmmakers made the decision to shoot *She's Gotta Have It* in black and white with Super 16mm film. Using black and white film was an aesthetic decision made by Dickerson and Lee. Super 16mm film, which has a wider picture area than regular 16mm film, was chosen to keep the costs down and to allow an eventual blow-up to 35mm for theatrical release.

A FAMILY FILM

The film became a family affair as Lee's sister Joie was cast as the former roommate of the lead character, Nola. His brother David provided black and white stills which were used throughout the film, and his father Bill Lee composed the jazz score. Lee even cast himself in the comedic role of Brooklyn born homeboy, "Mars Blackmon" — a character that continued beyond the film in TV commercials for basketball shoes.

THE FINAL BUDGET WAS $175,000

After 12 arduous days of shooting, the film was ready for post production. Editing of the film took place in Lee's apartment. He continued to raise money to complete his movie during this time by screening rough cuts to potential investors. With bill collectors literally closing in, Lee raced to finish the film in time for submission to the Cannes Film Festival in France. Despite financial hardships, the project was completed with a total budget of $175,000. *She's Gotta Have It* went on to be accepted into the Cannes Film Festival, one of the largest international events of its kind, held each year in France.

A BIG HIT ON THE FESTIVAL CIRCUIT

Prior to the festival at Cannes, Lee invited several small film distribution companies to the world premiere of *She's Gotta Have It* at the 1986 San Francisco Film Festival. During the screening, a power blackout occurred and interrupted the film. Lee grabbed a chair, sat on the dark stage, and fielded questions from the enthusiastic audience. The distributors were excited as well because they quickly submitted bids for the film. Lee selected Island Pictures as his distributor and they gave him $475,000 for the rights to the film.

During the summer of 1986, *She's Gotta Have It* became an instant hit at the Cannes Film Festival with the international audience of moviegoers and critics. The film won the "Prix du Film Jeunesse," a prize awarded to new films by first time directors at the festival.

SLAPPED WITH AN "X" RATING

Before its release in the U.S. the film hit a bit of a snag. The movie ratings organization, The Motion Picture Association of America (MPAA), found it to be, in their words, "saturated with sex." The film was given an "X" rating which is usually associated with pornography. (The MPAA, it should be noted, selects a group of parents to judge the content of films with regard to viewing by children.) Unwilling to accept an "X" rating, Lee made a slight edit to one of the love scenes, cutting out approximately two seconds of footage, and the film went on to receive an "R" rating. Lee found the MPAA's initial rating to be quite harsh compared to other films which had contained more sex than his. He attributed their reaction to an inability to deal with black sexuality on the screen, a rarity prior to his film.

$8 MILLION DOLLARS LATER

She's Gotta Have It went on to become a big hit for both Lee and his distributor Island Pictures as it made over eight million dollars. The success of his first movie quickly provided Lee with a deal to direct his next project for Island. This time he would helm a multi-million dollar film based upon his experiences at Morehouse College, called *School Daze.*

Note to the reader: For a full account on the making of *She's Gotta Have It,* I recommend that you read Spike Lee's book *Spike Lee's Gotta Have It: Inside Guerrilla Filmmaking,* published by Simon & Shuster, 1987.

2 Hollywood Shuffle

Robert Townsend: Co-Writer/Producer/Director/Actor

(Samuel Goldwyn, 1987)

THE SECOND FILM OF THE NEW JACK ERA

In 1987 one year after the release of *She's Gotta Have It*, Hollywood found another film made with the independent, New Jack spirit shown by Spike Lee. The movie was called *Hollywood Shuffle* and it marked the directorial debut of actor/comedian Robert Townsend. Like Lee's first film, Townsend crafted a perceptive comedy depicting a facet of the contemporary African American experience. His movie chronicled the travails of actor "Bobbie Taylor," played by Townsend, and his frustrating search for meaningful roles as a black actor.

A STORY BORN OUT OF FRUSTRATION

Townsend and fellow actor/comedian Keenan Ivory Wayans wrote the story for *Shuffle* based upon their personal experiences as struggling actors in Hollywood. After arriving in Los Angeles in 1982 from New York, Townsend found that the acting jobs open to him were very often limited to stereotyped renditions of criminals, slaves, and jive-talking characters. He would later parody this painful reality in his film *Hollywood Shuffle*.

HIS ACTING CAREER BEGAN AT 16

Because they lived in a rough area, on the West Side of Chicago, Townsend's mother kept him in the house most of the time and as a result, young Townsend watched a great deal of television. He soon developed a flair for mimicry as he would imitate actors in their movie roles for his friends. Townsend eventually became so good at his impressions that both his friends and his mother encouraged him to pursue a career in acting. He was also interested in becoming a professional basketball player, but came to realize that he did not have the ability to play professionally. So, with the encouragement of his friends and family, Townsend began to study acting at the age of 16.

After auditioning for The Experimental Black Actors' Guild in Chicago, Townsend became the youngest addition to the group at the age of 16. He also worked as an extra in his first film, the 1974 coming of age story, *Cooley High.* The young actor had only two lines, but he played a role he knew well, that of a basketball player.

He would later land roles as an extra in other 1970s films with black casts like *Mahogany* and *The Wiz.* Townsend also exercised his comic ability during this time as a member of the famous Chicago improvisational troupe known as *Second City.*

ACTING IN THE BIG APPLE

During the late 1970s Townsend pursued his education in the classroom and on stage. After graduating from high school, he enrolled at Illinois State University as a Radio-TV-Communications major. Wanting to continue his acting career, Townsend made the decision to move to New York City. He continued his college studies by transferring from Illinois State to William Paterson College in New Jersey. He also became an acting student under the tutelage of Stella Adler in Manhattan. In addition, Townsend joined the Negro Ensemble Company of New York and remained with them for two years.

To be closer to his acting commitments, Townsend would later transfer from William Paterson to Hunter College in New York. Eventually he dropped out of school in order to devote himself full-time to acting. While seeking acting jobs, he also made the rounds of the local comedy clubs to try out his stand-up routine. In 1980 he had the opportunity to audition for the comedy television show *Saturday Night Live,* but the position went instead to another young comedian named Eddie Murphy.

During his years in New York, Townsend was also able to find roles in TV commercials. After earning about $30,000 from a national soft drink commercial, he bought video equipment to tape performances of both himself and his friends, one of whom was his *Hollywood Shuffle* co-writer, Keenan Ivory Wayans.

THE MOVE TO HOLLYWOOD

In 1982 Robert Townsend loaded up a truck with all his belongings and headed for Hollywood to pursue a movie career. He went without a substantial role for about six months until he was cast in *A Soldier's Story* (1984) as a jeep driver. While acting in movies like *Streets of Fire, American Flyers,* and *A Soldier's Story,* he began to observe what was going on behind the camera. By asking questions of the crew members, Townsend learned what it would take to someday direct his own film.

MAKING A FILM WITH CREDIT CARDS

By 1984 Townsend was frustrated and unsatisfied with many of the demeaning movie roles available to him, so he made the decision to direct his own film. Using money from several of his acting jobs, he began production on a project co-written with fellow comedian Keenan Ivory Wayans called *Hollywood Shuffle.* The title referred to how Townsend felt when he was "shuffling" around Hollywood auditioning for terrible parts.

To get things started, he and Keenan Ivory Wayans gathered enough funds to shoot a black and white, five-minute short film called *Sam Ace: Death of a Breakdancer.* The film was a detective parody in which Townsend's character "Sam Ace" pursued the death of a break dancer named "Cookie-head Jenkins." The murderer "Jerri-curl" played by Wayans is defeated by Sam Ace after his jerri-curl activator is taken away from him, thus destroying his hairdo.

Townsend went on to use about $60,000 of his own money, plus filmstock donated from other filmmakers, to continue shooting vignettes. When the funds were low he used several credit cards to pay for production costs. By the time he finished the film, Townsend's credit card bills amounted to almost $40,000 worth of expenses.

As an independent director, Townsend found creative ways to get the scenes he wanted. Unable to afford official permits to shoot on the streets of Los Angeles, he bought tee-shirts from the University of California at Los Angeles (UCLA). If he was caught by the police Townsend would then use the shirts to support his claim that he was shooting a student film. Due to the fear of being kicked off the streets, he would often shoot a scene in one take, then move on to the next location. To save time and money, Townsend shot many of the interior scenes in his own apartment. Given that he could only shoot when he had money, the film took about two years to complete.

A JOB OFFER FROM EDDIE MURPHY

Actor/comedian Eddie Murphy saw a rough cut of *Hollywood Shuffle* and was impressed with the work in progress. Murphy then offered Townsend his second directing job on the documentary/concert film, *Eddie Murphy Raw* (1987). But before Townsend could start the project he had to get *Shuffle* into movie theaters.

ONE LAST CREDIT CARD GAMBLE

After 14 days of shooting, over the course of two years, with a final cost of $100,000 of Townsend's hard earned money, *Hollywood Shuffle* was ready to be seen. In a bold move he used his credit cards one last time to rent a theater to screen his film for potential distributors. He invited representatives from all of the major studios. Fortunately for Townsend, the Samuel Goldwyn Company not only agreed to distribute his film, but also to pay off his large credit card bills.

One month after its release the film grossed an estimated $850,000, which was rather good considering what the project cost to make. *Hollywood Shuffle* would go on to pull in approximately $7 million dollars at the box office.

AFTER SHUFFLE, TOWNSEND IS IN DEMAND

In 1987 at the age of 29, Robert Townsend had established himself as a successful director with *Hollywood Shuffle.* His second film *Eddie Murphy Raw* (1987) would solidify his reputation in Hollywood as it was highly successful at the box office. *Raw* eventually became the number one performance documentary to date with a total U.S. box office gross of $50 million.

Townsend followed up his successful work in movies with a series of hit comedy specials that he produced and hosted for the cable network HBO called *Robert Townsend and His Partners In Crime.* The specials, hosted by Townsend, featured him and many of his comedian friends in television and movie parodies. During the late 1980s he also had the opportunity to briefly host the network program *The Late Show* on Fox Television. Townsend was one of many guest hosts, including Arsenio Hall, who filled in after the departure of the original host, comedian Joan Rivers.

THE LONG WAIT FOR TOWNSEND'S THIRD FILM

Moviegoers looking forward to Townsend's next film had to wait at least three years. He was determined to spend ample time researching and developing a project with his writing partner, Keenan Ivory Wayans. Their project was a film about a fictional musical group called *The Five Heartbeats*.

3 School Daze

Spike Lee: Writer/Producer/Director/Actor

(Columbia Pictures, 1988)

A CONTROVERSIAL SECOND FILM

Two years had elapsed between the release of Spike Lee's first film *She's Gotta Have It* and his second, *School Daze*. Lee adapted the story from an earlier screenplay called *Homecoming,* which he wrote after graduating from New York University. In *School Daze* Lee incorporated four years of his experiences at the historically black college Morehouse into one film about a fictional school "Mission College." As a central issue, Lee used a conflict between light-skinned and dark-skinned black students as a vehicle to deal with the prejudices exhibited by some African Americans. Lee dramatized the problem in the form of a musical.

ISLAND PICTURES DROPS DAZE

Island Pictures, the distributor of Lee's first film and the backers of his second, had established a budget of $4 million for *Daze,* but they began to have concerns over both the potentially controversial subject matter and the size of the film. During the preproduction planning in January of 1987, Island executives asked Lee to make changes in the script to bring it within their budget limit of $4 million. Lee refused to reduce his vision of the film and Island Pictures informed him that they would not proceed with the project.

COLUMBIA TO THE RESCUE

Lee did not waste time finding a new home for his film. He had his lawyer Loretha Jones persuade her boss attorney Arthu r Klein who had contacts in Hollywood, to give the *School Daze* screenplay to Columbia Pictures. Approximately 24 hours after Island Pictures terminated the project, David Picker, head of production at Columbia, read Lee's script and made a deal to finance the film. Picker was looking for small, independent films like Lee's for Columbia's new studio head at the time, David Puttnam. Puttman, a former independent filmmaker who won the 1981 Best Picture Academy Award for his film *Chariots of Fire,* wanted to develop small, quality projects at Columbia. The studio gave Lee a budget of $6.5 million and the director continued with his plans to shoot the film at his alma mater Morehouse in Atlanta.

LEE GETS KICKED OFF CAMPUS

Cameras began to roll on the production of *School Daze* during March of 1987. The locations included the four college campuses that made up the Atlanta University Center (AUC), Spelman, Morehouse, Clark, and Morris Brown. After four weeks of shooting, Lee received a letter from a lawyer representing the AUC telling him to submit his script for review by the college presidents. Lee refused to release his screenplay. He was then asked to stop shooting on the AUC premises. The college presidents were apparently concerned that *School Daze* would present a negative image of black colleges. After the AUC halted production on their property, Lee resumed shooting at Atlanta University, the only school that had signed a written contract.

RACIAL TENSION BETWEEN CAST MEMBERS

Lee created a sense of tension between the two major female factions in the movie. He housed the dark-skinned "Jigaboos" as they were called in the film, in a hotel separate from the light-skinned "Wannabees", a word used in the movie meaning "wannabee white." Some of the cast members complained that the light-skinned women were given preferential treatment on the set and better hotel accommodations. During a "Greek" dance sequence, the two groups reportedly exchanged improvised derisive remarks steeped in racial prejudice.

THE BEGINNING OF AN ENSEMBLE

Only two performers from Lee's first film, *She's Gotta Have It,* were cast in *School Daze:* the director himself and his sister, Joie. Lee portrayed "Half-Pint," a virginal young man who was one of several pledges to the "Gamma Phi Gamma" fraternity. His sister Joie was cast as one of the "Jigaboos." Joie, along with some of the other actors in the film, would continue to be featured in several of Spike

Lee's subsequent movies. Among those in *School Daze* who would later have larger roles in Lee's films were Bill Nunn, "Grady," who would return in *Do The Right Thing,* and *Mo' Better Blues.* Samuel L. Jackson, who portrayed a local yokel in Daze, would have parts in *Do The Right Thing, Mo' Better Blues* and *Jungle Fever.* Giancarlo Esposito, "Julian," a.k.a "Big Brother Almighty," would appear in *Do The Right Thing, Mo' Better Blues,* and as an assassin in *Malcolm X.*

A VICTIM OF NEW MANAGEMENT

While Lee was completing production of *School Daze,* the two men directly responsible for supporting the film at Columbia Pictures, executive David Picker and studio head David Puttnam, were ousted from their jobs. Puttnam's replacement, Dawn Steel, like most newly appointed Hollywood studio heads, refused to support her predecessor's work, which included Lee's *Daze.*

As a result of the new management, Lee was told that Columbia would be spending very little money to advertise his film. The studio made it clear that it would not provide national television advertising. Instead of marketing the film through the traditional routes, primarily magazines and television, Columbia showed its reluctance to spend money on the project by asking Lee to travel across the country, to visit many cities, during a two-week promotional tour.

Ironically, *School Daze* quickly became a top money earner for Columbia Pictures when it was released in February of 1988 in just over 200 theaters. By the end of the year, *Daze* grossed over $15 million despite the studio's sparse marketing campaign. It also proved to be Columbia's only profitable film in 1988.

The film was successful not only in theaters, but in record stores and in dance clubs. The homecoming dance number in the film spawned both a hit record from the soundtrack, "Da Butt," and a popular dance invented by Lee of the same name.

LEE DOES THE RIGHT THING

After completing *School Daze* Lee was anxious to continue his momentum by quickly launching another film. Having brought the subject of color prejudice among African Americans out into the open in *Daze,* he would now turn his attention to a story about race relations on a larger scale in New York City with a script entitled *Do The Right Thing.*

Note to the reader: For a full account on the making of *School Daze,* I recommend that you read Spike Lee's book *Uplift The Race: The Construction of School Daze* by Spike Lee with Lisa Jones, published by Simon & Schuster, 1988.

4 I'm Gonna Git You Sucka

Keenan Ivory Wayans: Writer/Director/Actor

(United Artists, 1988)

WAYANS DOES SHUFFLE WITH TOWNSEND

Keenan Ivory Wayans' 1988 directorial debut *I'm Gonna Git You Sucka* was not his first encounter with filmmaking. A year earlier a film he co-wrote with Robert Townsend, *Hollywood Shuffle,* was released. Much of the praise for the film went to Townsend, but Wayans was a crucial part of the production team from the start. He and Townsend scripted a five-minute, black and white detective spoof called *Sam Ace: Death of a Breakdancer.* The short film starred Townsend as Sam Ace and Wayans as "Jerri Curl," the killer of a breakdancer named "Cookie-Head Jenkins." Sam Ace later became a part of *Hollywood Shuffle* after Townsend raised enough money to shoot six additional vignettes over the course of two years.

Wayans and Townsend continued their partnership after Shuffle when they co-wrote Eddie Murphy's concert film Raw (1987) and the HBO cable special *Robert Townsend and His Partners in Crime* (1987). Both Raw and the HBO special, which was later expanded into a series of shows, were extremely successful ventures for both Wayans and Townsend. However, Wayans longed to create his own project without the help of his close friends, Murphy and Townsend.

A $3 MILLION BUDGET FOR HIS FIRST FILM

The initial idea for *I'm Gonna Git You Sucka,* a parody of the black action film heroes of the 1970s, has been attributed to Eddie Murphy, but Wayans scripted the film despite the fact that Murphy and Townsend wanted to help finance and write the film with him. After the success of *Hollywood Shuffle* Wayans was determined to break free from the emerging shadow of his partner Robert Townsend to make a film on his own.

Several movie studios expressed interest in the *Sucka* screenplay, but only if Wayans made changes, including the addition of white characters. One studio told him that perhaps a white actor should be cast as an adopted brother who thinks he is black. Wayans resisted such suggestions and instead signed a deal with United Artists (UA) because the studio agreed to use his script without changes and gave him a budget of $3 million.

Wayans, in addition to serving as director of *Sucka,* cast himself in the lead role as "Jack Spade," a cowardly veteran who returns home after the death of his brother "June Bug" who had met his demise from wearing too many gold chains. His brother also worked for a white man named "Mr. Big" who's henchmen sought to collect June Bug's debts by threatening Jack's family. Jack then enlists the aid of his heroes from the past to rid the neighborhood of Mr. Big.

For the aging heroes Wayans assembled a supporting cast of performers from the ranks of older black film stars, including football legend Jim Brown, veteran actor Bernie Casey, actor/musician Isaac Hayes, a TV character actor from the 1970s — Antonio Fargas ("Huggy Bear" from *Starsky and Hutch),* and one of TV's first black detectives Clarence Williams III, better known to audiences as "Link" from the late 1960s show, *The Mod Squad.*

UA TRIES TO BURY *SUCKA*

Once *Sucka* was finished, UA scheduled a December 2, 1988 opening date during the competitive Christmas movie season. Wayans has commented about his suspicion that the studio, lacking confidence in his all-black movie and seeking to cut its losses early, tried to bury *Sucka* by releasing it against big budget holiday films. He found their marketing strategy to be inadequate as UA used cartoon-like art for the movie posters and reportedly spent very little money on advertising. In fact, UA released the film mainly in predominantly black cities like Washington, D.C., Baltimore, and Chicago. Despite the studio's apparent mishandling of the marketing, moviegoers managed to find the film. *I'm Gonna Git You Sucka* went on to gross over $15 million in U.S. theaters, thus returning quite a profit to the studio, given its initial $3 million budget.

AN OFFER HE COULDN'T REFUSE

In an effort to secure a deal for his next film project, Wayans invited studio executives from 20th Century Fox to attend a screening of *Sucka.* His movie studio guests never arrived. However, executives from Fox Television did, and they promptly offered Wayans an opportunity to create a half-hour show for their struggling new network. Initially Wayans was reluctant to work in television because his heart was set on directing movies, but the offer by Fox was too good to pass up as they gave him creative control to develop any kind of show that he wanted.

THE CREATION OF *IN LIVING COLOR*

Wayans quickly went to work and created a comedy show called *In Living Color,* which premiered during the summer of 1990. The show featured a predominantly black cast including his sister Kim, brothers Damon, Shawn and later, Marlon. An older brother by two years, Dwayne, also served as a production assistant. The show was soon a Sunday night hit for Fox and went on to earn its share of awards, including television's top honor, the "Emmy."

THE WAYANS, A FAMILY OF TEN

The casting of his family members for *In Living Color* could be viewed as more than just nepotism by Wayans. His upbringing in New York City as the second oldest of a close knit, poor family of ten children, perhaps influenced his hiring decisions. The patriarch of the Wayans clan Howell Wayans was a strict father. Howell, along with his wife Elvira, struggled to support their large family on his small salary as a supermarket manager. The Wayans lived in poverty and were relegated to substandard public housing commonly referred to as "the projects." Keenan did his share of pitching in to help the family. By the time he was 16, Wayans held a full-time job as a manager of a fast food restaurant, while attending high school.

FROM COLLEGE TO STAND-UP COMEDIAN

In spite of working long hours after school, Wayans received a scholarship to attend Tuskegee Institute in Alabama to study engineering. While in college he harbored an interest in becoming a comedian. Wayans had developed the desire to pursue comedy at an early age. When he was about six years old he saw Richard Pryor perform on a television show. Young Wayans was so enthralled with Pryor's ability to make an audience laugh that he decided that comedy was the career for him. The need to perform, to reach an audience with laughter became so strong that Wayans left Tuskegee one semester before graduation to try his hand in the comedy clubs of New York.

He soon began to find work as a stand-up comedian in venues like the Improv, albeit for little money, often earning no more than $20 per appearance. Wayans also began meeting other up and coming comedians working in New York, including Robert Townsend. In 1978 at the age of 19 he met another young comedian, a 16 year old named Eddie Murphy, backstage at the Improv. That chance meeting between the aspiring stand-up comedians would grow into a friendship that would continue across country after Keenan made his next big move, this time to Los Angeles.

STRUGGLING IN L.A.

In 1980 Wayans moved to L.A. to pursue a career in acting. When auditioning for movies and TV roles, the aspiring actor found he wasn't "black enough," according to some casting directors. They were looking to fill stereotyped portrayals of African Americans. When the acting roles weren't forthcoming, he returned to stand-up comedy by making appearances at clubs like the Improv and the Comedy Store. By 1981, things began to pick up career-wise as he landed a few small roles on NBC sitcoms.

It was during the early 1980s that Wayans began to turn to writing because of the scarcity of substantial acting roles for blacks. He also teamed up with his longtime friend and fellow comedian/actor Robert Townsend during this period. The duo developed comedy routines together, and they went on to co-write *Hollywood Shuffle.*

WAYANS RETURNS TO THE MOVIES

With his immensely popular TV show *In Living Color* going strong after several seasons, Wayans began to take a back seat in terms of performing on the program so that he could return to feature films. During 1992 he had his second film in development, in which he would serve as both actor and director, entitled *Lloyd of London.* The story was about a black police officer from England, who pursues a suspect to the U.S., and teams up with a Washington, D.C. cop played by Wayans.

By the end of 1992 Wayans became totally free to pursue his movie career as he left the show he created, *In Living Color,* over a dispute with Fox Television. Fox began to air episodes from *In Living*

Color's first season without consulting with Wayans. Reportedly, Wayans believed that Fox was diluting the future earning potential of the show by repeating early episodes. His reasoning was centered around the concern that viewers may not want to see repeat episodes in the future if they were shown prematurely on the network. The early episodes in essence would lose their rarity if they were shown repeatedly.

After leaving *In Living Color* Keenan Ivory Wayans continued to develop movie projects during the early 1990s. Among the scripts he was pursuing with Hollywood studios was his cop comedy *Lloyd of London* and another comedy called *Blankman* about a poor superhero which was to star his brother, rising movie star Damon Wayans.

5 Do The Right Thing

Spike Lee: Writer/Producer/Director/Actor

(Universal, 1989)

HIS MOST CONTROVERSIAL FILM TO DATE

Spike Lee was determined to quickly follow-up his second film *School Daze* in an effort to take advantage of his successful track record. Drawing inspiration from a tragic event at that time, known as "The Howard Beach Incident," named after the area of New York City in which a black teenager died as the result of a police choke hold, Lee fashioned a screenplay in just 15 days called *Do The Right Thing*. In the script he tackled the volatile subject of race relations in New York City.

The screenplay, which was to become his most controversial to date, presented a fictional story of the hottest day of the year and the effect it has on one neighborhood. The heat and racial tension combine to build toward a confrontation when a disgruntled teen, "Buggin' Out" (Giancarlo Esposito), leads a boycott against pizzeria owner "Sal" (Danny Aiello) for his unwillingness to put pictures of famous African Americans on his "Wall of Fame." Buggin' Out's friend "Radio Raheem" (Bill Nunn) joins the protest and refuses to turn off his blaring radio in the pizzeria, which prompts a fight with Sal. The police then arrive and restrain Radio Raheem in a choke hold with a night stick, which inadvertently kills him.

"Mookie" (Spike Lee), a care-free pizza delivery man, reacts to the murder of his friend by throwing a garbage can through the window of Sal's storefront. This action provokes a crowd of neighborhood teens to vandalize and burn Sal's pizzeria. By the end of the film we find that truly no one has done the "right thing."

LEE LOOKS FOR SUPPORTIVE STUDIO

Coming off a bad experience with Columbia Pictures, with his second film *School Daze*, Lee was determined to find the right home for his next project. When he approached Paramount Pictures with his screenplay, they raised objections to the ending and asked for changes which would make it less inflammatory. Lee quickly moved on to Universal Pictures which agreed to make his film "as is" without any changes to the script.

LESSONS LEARNED WITH *DAZE*

With *Do The Right Thing Lee* applied many of the things he learned during his experience working on *School Daze* to prevent potential trouble. First, he refused to sign a deal with Paramount Pictures because they had reservations about both his script and the budget. Lee had a similar experience with Island Pictures which originally agreed to finance *Daze,* but pulled out at the last minute as they were unwilling to financially support what they believed to be a controversial script.

With regard to negotiating contracts, Lee had learned to get all agreements in writing. A lack of contracts caused him to lose his locations during the shooting of *Daze.* Lee also fought to have "final cut" (the director's edited version of the film) on *Do The Right Thing* so that he could have control over the content of his work.

THE $6.5 MILLION BUDGET FIGHT

The logistics of using an ensemble cast, a union crew and New York City locations all became factors in the budgeting process of *Right Thing.* Lee and his line producer, John Kilik originally arrived at a $10 million figure, but after Paramount Pictures declined, based upon both the subject matter of the script and the cost, the two then reduced the budget to $7.5 million for Universal. The studio wanted Lee to further reduce the expenses and even suggested that he shoot some of the film in Hollywood where the costs of shooting on the studio lot would be cheaper. Lee wanted to stay in New York to give the film an authentic look so he agreed to a $6.5 million offer by Universal. This was a tight budget considering everything the director had to accomplish in a shooting schedule of roughly eight and a half weeks.

THE PRODUCTION RUNS SMOOTHLY

Lee shot the film from July 18, 1988 to September 9, 1988 on one block in the Bedford-Stuyvesant section of Brooklyn, New York. Shooting proceeded without major incident and the weather, for the most part, cooperated with a majority of sunny days. Upon its completion, Lee submitted the film to the Cannes Film Festival in France and received acceptance into the festival on his birthday, March 20, 1989, just as he did three years earlier with his first film *She's Gotta Have It.*

SECOND TIME AT CANNES IS NO CHARM

The reaction to Lee's film at Cannes was mixed. Some critics saw it as his best work, others had problems with the ending of the film. When his film failed to win the top honor at the festival Lee felt robbed of the prize, based upon a statement reportedly made by the president of the festival jury, German filmmaker, Wim Wenders. Wenders, according to Lee, suggested that character "Mookie", played by Lee, was "unheroic" for throwing the garbage can through the pizzeria window. Lee found the comment ironic as the winning film, *Sex, Lies and Videotape,* featured as its main character a man who interviewed women, and then masturbated as they described their sexual experiences.

PRESS ANTICIPATES VIOLENCE OVER LEE'S ENDING

Prior to the film's release, the press and several movie critics issued dire warnings about *Do The Right Thing.* Several reviewers predicted that Lee's film might incite violence among black teenagers because of both the riot scene and the supposedly threatening Malcolm X quote at the end of the movie. Specifically, *New York* magazine columnist Joe Klein argued that *Do The Right Thing* might cause violence and ruin David Dinkins' chances at becoming mayor of New York City. "If Lee does hook large black audiences," wrote Klein, "there's a good chance the message they take from the film will increase racial tensions in the city. If they act violently — which can't be ruled out — the candidate with the most to lose will be David Dinkins." *(New York,* "The City Politic: Spiked?," June 26, 1989, p.14).

In the same issue of the magazine, critic David Denby claimed that an artist whose point of view is coherent should not be held responsible if some of his audience misunderstand his work. Spike Lee, he suggested, did not have a coherent point of view and therefore warned, "The end of this movie is a shambles, and if some audiences go wild, he's partly responsible." *(New York,* "He's Gotta Have It," June 26, 1989, p. 54).

Lee responded to both articles with a letter to the magazine's editor in which he accused the authors of stereotyping black teens by suggesting that only their white readership would be able to act responsibly after seeing the film. Lee wrote, "Are we to conclude that only whites are intellectually and morally endowed to tackle an issue as complex as race relations in New York City?" *(New York,* Letters: Spike Lee Replies: 'Say It Ain't So, Joe,' July 17, 1989, p.6).

TEENS DO THE RIGHT THING

The film was released on June 30, 1989 and during its theatrical run no incidents of violence were reported. Contrary to predictions of critics and the media, who cautioned white moviegoers that the film would possibly incite riots, African American teens behaved responsibly. Lee has pointed out that none of the reviewers offered a retraction, apology, or follow-up to their warnings about his film.

A PROFITABLE FILM, DESPITE THE NEGATIVE PRESS

The debate over the potential violent reaction to Lee's film generated probably the most press of all his movies up to that time. Many of the stories could be viewed as negative, given the focus on possible outbreaks of violence. While those reports may have deterred many white moviegoers from attending the film, *Do The Right Thing* made a sizable profit at the box office, grossing over $28 million with an original cost of $6.5 million.

LEE'S FIRST ACADEMY AWARD NOMINATION

Unlike many of the critics who condemned *Do The Right Thing* before its release, a number of reviewers gave the movie high praise. Specifically, the performances of Lee and Danny Aiello were singled out for their excellence along with the vibrant colorful cinematography of Ernest Dickerson. The film made the top ten list of many reviewers, Dickerson won the 1989 Film Critics Award for cinematography, and both Lee and Aiello received Academy Award nominations for "Best Original Screenplay" and "Best Supporting Actor", respectively. Unfortunately for Lee and Aiello, neither man took home an Academy Award. The awards instead went to the movie *Dead Poet's Society* and actor Denzel Washington for his role in *Glory*.

On March 26, 1990, during the 62nd Annual Academy Awards ceremony, actress/award presenter Kim Basinger ignored her scripted comments and chided the Academy on-air, during the live broadcast, for not recognizing Lee's film for the "Best Picture" honor.

THE "BEST ACTRESS" DIDN'T SEE HIS FILM

Appearing on the late-night news program *Nightline* after the ceremony, Lee along with film critic Gene Siskel and actor/director Dennis Hopper discussed the apparent bias among Academy members when it came to nominating an outspoken, black man like Lee. Siskel revealed that backstage during the ceremony he asked 80 year-old actress and Academy member Jessica Tandy, who won that night for "Best Actress," to compare race relations in her film, the period piece *Driving Miss Daisy* (the story of an elderly white woman and her black chauffeur), to that of Lee's contemporary view in *Do The Right Thing.* Tandy replied that she had not seen Lee's film. Lee and Siskel found her action ironic given the fact that Universal sent a video cassette copy of the film to every Academy member. Lee and Siskel surmised, perhaps more voters, like Tandy, did not even bother to watch the film before voting for "Best Picture." This was due, in part, as suggested by Siskel, to the make-up of the people casting ballots for the Academy: older, white, politically conservative and wealthy. Dennis Hopper pointed out that with the awards, directors vote for directors and writers for writers, whereas just about all of the membership can vote for "Best Picture." It was the progressive writers, argued Hopper, that gave Lee his nomination for "Best Original Screenplay."

HIS FIRST FILM OF THE 1990s

While promoting *Do The Right Thing,* Spike Lee began to develop the script for his next project. Lee wanted to begin the 1990s by stepping back from his usual controversial stories, to create a film which featured jazz and male/female relationships. The working title of the film was *A Love Supreme* taken from the title of a jazz album by artist John Coltrane, and the star was to be one of the top black actors in the industry, Academy Award winning leading man, Denzel Washington.

Note to the reader: For a full account on the making of *Do The Right Thing,* I recommend that you read Spike Lee's book of the same title by Spike Lee with Lisa Jones, published by Simon and Schuster, 1989.

6 House Party

Reginald and Warrington Hudlin: Writer/Director and Producer, respectively

(New Line Cinema, 1990)

A SIBLING PARTNERSHIP

A number of significant partnerships were forged during the 1980s between African American filmmakers. Among the famous collaborators, several stand-out: Spike Lee & Ernest Dickerson, Robert Townsend & Keenan Ivory Wayans, and Doug McHenry & George Jackson. By 1990 another team joined the ranks of filmmaking duos; siblings Reginald and Warrington Hudlin. The two arrived on the major motion picture scene with a partnership grounded in the kinship of brotherhood. They were better known as "The Hudlin Brothers." The manner in which Reginald and Warrington referred to themselves, as simply The Hudlin Brothers, pointed to the closeness of their working relationship as they often took turns producing or directing their joint projects.

NO OVERNIGHT SUCCESS FOR THESE BROTHERS

In 1990 the Hudlin Brothers received critical raves and box office success for their first feature film *House Party*, a comedy about a teenager's quest to attend the biggest house party of the year. The success the Hudlins achieved with their first major film was not of the overnight variety. These brothers were from the tough streets of East St. Louis, Missouri, and they went on to Ivy league schools and became independent filmmakers. The younger of the two, Reggie, went to Harvard while his older brother Warrington attended Yale University. Warrington credits legendary dancer Kathryn Dunham for helping him get a full scholarship from a St. Louis foundation to attend Yale. As a teenager Warrington came to know Dunham as he had the opportunity to learn how to play the drums at her Performing Arts Training Center.

ONE BROTHER WENT TO YALE ...

While at Yale, Warrington developed a desire to deal with social issues through film after attending a screening of Melvin Van Peebles' landmark film, *Sweet Sweetback's Baadasssss Song* (1971). After graduating from Yale, Warrington went on to make a number of documentaries including the 1974 film *Black At Yale*, which dealt with his experiences at the predominantly white institution. One of his most successful short films *Street Corner Stories*, an observational, documentary examination of street corner conversations, was translated into several languages and distributed widely in Europe.

... THE OTHER ATTENDED HARVARD

Reggie Hudlin, having grown up watching his older brother make movies, followed Warrington's lead and went on to study filmmaking at Harvard University. Although he was trained in the documentary tradition, Reggie showed a flair for fiction and comedy as evidenced by his early works. One of his films, entitled *Reggie's World of Soul* (1985), was a monologue delivered by a man who wants to market a clenched fist, found on afro picks, as a design element on other products such as spatulas and back-scratchers. A year later he made *The Kold Waves* (1986), a short film about a white kid who wants to join an all-black band. Each of these films dealt with serious subjects, shot with an almost documentary-like style, but were told with a comic, satirical edge.

THE ORIGINAL VERSION OF HOUSE PARTY

Reggie's final college project, his thesis film, exemplified his ability to deal with real characters and situations within a humorous context. His 20 minute student film was called *House Party*. Reggie was inspired to write the script after hearing a song by Luther Vandross on the radio called "Bad Boy/Having a Party." In the song, Vandross recounted the tale of a young man preparing for a house party. The young filmmaker could relate to the song as he attended house parties back in East St. Louis as a young man. In Reggie's script a teenager wants to join his friends at a party, but his father, a single parent, fears that his son will get into some sort of trouble. Specifically, he's afraid the boy will father a child at an early age as he once did.

WARRINGTON INTERVIEWS REGGIE

In 1986, years before the Hudlin brothers became famous, they had the opportunity to discuss their early work on *Black Film Focus,* a program which aired on a New York-based PBS affiliate. Warrington co-hosted with music critic Nelson George. On the show, Warrington interviewed his younger brother and they discussed his films, *Reggie's World of Soul* and *House Party*. Reggie pointed out that his work as a filmmaker was inspired by music, specifically, the rhythm, culture, and social messages found in funk and hip-hop. He went on to point out that professional performers were not used in his films because he wanted to bring a freshness to the dialogue that non-actors could provide.

Reggie also discussed his desire to depict three-dimensional black teens and adults in *House Party* as he felt what he called "the burden of history" as a black filmmaker. African American moviegoers, he pointed out, often expected black films to embody every facet and nuance of their culture because historically speaking, very few major films were made by black filmmakers. With that burden in mind Reggie didn't want to present common, stereotyped portrayals of his characters.

WARRINGTON CREATES A FILMMAKER'S FOUNDATION

Warrington demonstrated his serious commitment to black cinema in 1978 by co-founding, with several friends, a non-profit organization called The Black Filmmaker Foundation (BFF). The foundation grew by leaps and bounds over the years and by 1992 had two offices, one in its original New York base, and the other located in the heart of the moviemaking community of Hollywood.

Today the BFF helps aspiring film and video makers in a number of ways including assistance with gathering funding, monthly screening of independent films, educational seminars led by industry professionals, and a monthly newsletter for over 1500 members.

THE HUDLINS BECOME A TEAM

Warrington and Reggie became a team in 1986 as they pooled their respective talents and began to work together. A mutual friend, who owned a small record company at the time, gave them the opportunity to direct music videos. As a team, the Hudlins would take turns as producer and director on different projects. As their collaboration grew, Reggie became the primary writer of the team.

"NO, MY BROTHER. YOU'VE GOT TO BUY YOUR OWN."

One of their joint efforts of 1986 went on to become a cult classic. Reggie and Warrington produced a TV commercial for a mail order album of romantic ballads called *Hey Love*. The 30 second spot became popular because of its humor. In the commercial a group of men and women are at a dull house party sitting around on a couch, when one of the men suggests that they play the *Hey Love* album. The couples begin to dance to slow love ballads and the party quickly becomes a hit. The lead actor in the commercial, John Canada Terrell, the vain suitor from Spike Lee's *She's Gotta Have It,* is asked by a friend if he can borrow the album. Terrell responds matter-of-factly, "No, my brother. You've got to buy your own." This closing tag line quickly became part of the black pop cultural lingo. In fact, the line later became a recurring joke in the Hudlins' feature film *House Party*.

THE HUDLINS HIT THE BIG TIME

In 1988 the Hudlins made the move up to major motion pictures. A small independent production and distribution company from New York, New Line Cinema, agreed to develop Reggie's feature length version of his thesis film *House Party*. New Line was attracted to Reggie's script because the company wanted to tie into the popularity of the rap music market. The script for the feature film *House Party* borrowed both the basic plot and a number of the actual lines from Reggie's earlier student film.

REGGIE CASTS HIS "FUNKADELIC" IDOL

With regard to casting, Reggie had a number of people in mind for certain roles. Legendary recording artist George Clinton, leader of the 1970s funk-psychedelic group "Parliament-Funkadelic," was given a cameo, playing a disc jockey at an outdoor party. Reggie grew up with Clinton's music and wanted to pay homage to the man that influenced his whole approach to film aesthetics. Clinton took bold experimental chances with his musical arrangements, infusing his lyrics with serious messages, and yet he had a profound sense of humor in everything he did.

KID N' PLAY TAKE THE LEADS

The lead roles of *House Party* went to a duo of up and coming rappers named "Kid N' Play." Christopher Reid, with his then trademark half-foot high, eraser-shaped hair style, was the "Kid" portion of the team and his friend Christopher Martin was "Play." Reggie caught an appearance by Kid N' Play on the cable network Black Entertainment Television (BET) where they referred to the Hudlin's *Hey Love* commercial by using the tag line, "No my brother. You've got to buy your own," in the course of conversation. They also pointed out that they wanted to star in movies. Reggie made note of their comic abilities and decided that the pair would be ideal for his film.

"Kid N' Play" went on to use their stage names in *House Party*. Kid portrayed the young man seeking to join a party planned by his friend Play. Comedian Robin Harris, who died at the age of 35 of a heart attack a week after the film's release (March 18, 1990), was cast as Play's strict, but caring, father. The rest of the cast was rounded out with a trio of rappers, named Full Force, who portrayed a group of high school bullies.

A FAST SHOOT IN HOLLYWOOD

With the cast in place and the film budgeted at $2.5 million by New Line Cinema, the Hudlins headed for the sound stages of Hollywood to shoot their film. Reggie signed on as the writer/director while Warrington served as producer on the film. Production moved along at a fast pace. Reggie often completed 20 camera setups (separate camera positions) each day, a great deal faster than most Hollywood directors.

PARTY IMPRESSES SUNDANCE CROWD

Before *House Party* hit the theaters, the Hudlins took their film to the Sundance United States Film Festival, an annual event organized by actor Robert Redford in Utah. The response to the film was extremely positive. The Hudlins found that the audience, which was predominantly white, really connected with the universal theme of teenagers trying to sneak out of the house to join their friends.

THIS HIT FILM WAS NO FLUKE

House Party's debut on March 9, 1990 became a quick favorite with audiences as it went on to earn a total of $27 million. Considering its original $2.5 million budget, the film was certainly a success at the box office. The success of *House Party* came as no great surprise to its creators, who fully realized that their film was not only a solid piece of entertainment, infused with social messages, but it also filled a void in the marketplace. The Hudlins have pointed out that the executives at New Line grossly underestimated the earning potential of their film because they compared it to the only other contemporary black film of that time, Spike Lee's, *She's Gotta Have It.* Like other movie executives, using precedent as their guidepost, New Line told the Hudlins that perhaps the film should open in only 300 theaters and would probably just make about $12 million, but the film went on to earn well over twice that amount.

HUDLINS RECEIVE SAFE SEX AWARD

House Party was not only popular with movie audiences, but with many critics as well because it offered a slice of black teen life that had never been presented on screen before. The film also contained an abstinence/safe sex message as the protagonist "Kid" decides to forgo a sexual encounter with his girlfriend, because he doesn't have a condom with him. The Center for Population Options gave the Hudlins an award for the safe-sex message contained in their film. The Hudlin brothers have often commented that they wanted to give their audience more than just a movie full of laughs. The filmmakers made a commitment to include responsible messages in their film because it was targeted for a teen audience.

AFRAID OF THE DARK IN DENVER

Not all was completely rosy for the release of *House Party.* Despite a positive response from the Sundance Festival and movie critics, Warrington recalled that one theater owner in Denver refused to turn down the lights while the movie was being screened. The owner apparently feared having a predominantly black audience in a darkened theater.

AFTER *PARTY,* THE HUDLINS ARE HOT

After the success of *House Party* the Hudlins found themselves very much in demand. Instead of simply cranking out another film, they signed several development deals including a contract with a television network and a three picture deal with Tri-Star pictures. As they were preparing their next collaboration, reportedly a science-fiction comedy, Eddie Murphy called on the team to head a project he was developing as a comeback of sorts, after a two year absence from the screen. The film Murphy wanted the Hudlin Brothers to direct and produce was to be called *Boomerang*.

7 Def By Temptation

James Bond III: Writer/Producer/Director/Actor

(Troma, 1990)

HIS NAME IS BOND ... JAMES BOND III

The first horror film to come from the new generation of black filmmakers was a 1990 production called *Def By Temptation.* The 26 year old writer, director, producer, and star of the film happened to be the same person, James Bond III. His name was advantageous as a conversation starter because of the movie character "secret agent 007, James Bond" known world-wide by moviegoers.

Bond's film *Def By Temptation,* a stylish vampire film with a keen sense of humor, offers the tale of a young divinity student, Joel (played by Bond), who is tempted by an attractive young woman. Unbeknownst to Joel, the seductive woman happens to be a bar hopping vampire who has a habit of getting men into bed, drinking their blood, and then promptly killing them. The title of the movie itself is a humorous play on words using the slang term "def" for both its sound, similar to "death," and its definition, loosely translated as something being extremely exciting--which applies to the female vampire in the film.

AN ALFRED HITCHCOCK IN THE MAKING

The distributor of the film, Troma Inc. (a small production company), declared in its promotional material that director James Bond III was "an Alfred Hitchcock in the making." That's high praise for a young director, but compared to the B-movies Troma was known for producing, such as *The Toxic Avenger, Sgt. Kabukiman, N.Y.P.D,* and *Surf Nazis Must Die,* Bond's film was easily superior to their usual product. It is important to note that Troma did not produce the film, but merely served as its distributor.

HIS CAREER BEGAN AS A CHILD ACTOR

James Bond III didn't arrive on the scene overnight in the entertainment industry. He started out as a child actor in network television. In 1977 Bond was chosen to be part of an ensemble cast for an NBC, Saturday morning children's program called *The Red Hand Gang.* The young actor portrayed an amateur detective on the show. The weekly series was scheduled opposite two hit shows on competing networks, Dick Clark's long running music show *American Bandstand* and Bill Cosby's animated creation, *Fat Albert and The Cosby Kids.* Against two established programs *The Red Hand Gang* didn't stand a chance and was canceled after a few months on the air.

THE FISH THAT SAVED PITTSBURGH

Several years later Bond would make his feature film debut in the 1979 comedy, *The Fish That Saved Pittsburgh.* He played Tyrone Millman, the water boy of a hapless Pittsburgh, Pennsylvania basketball team. In the film, Tyrone consults with a female astrologer and she transforms the basketball squad into winners by convincing the team's owner to select players according to one astrological sign, "Pisces, the fish." Thus, the "fish" go on to save Pittsburgh by winning a basketball championship. Despite the fact that *Fish* starred several veteran comedians, such as Flip Wilson and Jonathan Winters, as well as professional basketball stars Julius "Dr. J" Erving and Kareem Abdul-Jabbar, the movie was a rather weak comedy that failed at the box office.

ACTING IN *DAZE*

After *The Fish That Saved Pittsburgh,* Bond appeared on screen in only a few productions. Of note, he starred in a 1980 short drama called *The Sky is Gray.* Set in the racially segregated American South of the 1940s, the film presented Bond in the role of a boy who learns about prejudice firsthand as he leaves his sheltered community to travel to the heart of town in search of a dentist for his toothache.

Bond didn't appear again on screen in a major motion picture until 1988. He had a cameo in Spike Lee's second film, *School Daze.* Bond portrayed Monroe, a student attending the fictional black school, Mission College. The role provided only a few lines of dialogue, but Bond got more than just another acting job. A few years later he would work again with two people from *School Daze* as their director.

BOND WORKS WITH ERNEST DICKERSON

Bond's directorial debut, *Def By Temptation* contained a cast and crew mainly associated with other black filmmakers. Two of the lead characters, portrayed by actors Bill Nunn and Kadeem Hardison, appeared in films directed by Spike Lee ("Radio Raheem," *Do The Right Thing)* and Keenan Ivory Wayans (a thug, *I'm Gonna Git You Sucka),* respectively. Bond also established a major coup by getting Spike Lee's longtime collaborator, cinematographer Ernest Dickerson, to photograph his film. This made the low-budget *Def* appear to be more expensive than it actually was.

TEMPTATION OPENS IN ONE CITY AT A TIME

Def By Temptation opened in a handful of theaters during the summer of 1990, and often played in a city for only a few weeks before moving on. The distributor Troma simply did not have the financing to promote the movie on a larger scale, but many critics began to take notice of this unique horror film made with an all-black cast. The film found greater success on home video and especially on television as it played on cable television movie channels well into 1991.

BOND TAKES TO THE STAGE

Following the release of *Def By Temptation* James Bond III was ready to move on to bigger and better projects. After the release of *Def* he had a development deal with Columbia television to produce an all-black situation comedy, but the project never came to fruition as a viable television show. So, just as suddenly as he burst on to the scene as a director, after an almost ten year hiatus from the movies, James Bond III remained inactive in the movie industry during the early 1990s. Instead, he tackled yet another part of the entertainment industry — live theater. After starting out as a child actor, then directing his first film while in his early 20s, James Bond III now turned his attention to the stage as he mounted his own theatrical production in New York City.

8 Mo' Better Blues

Spike Lee: Writer/Producer/Director/Actor

(Universal, 1990)

WHAT DOES "MO' BETTER" MEAN ANYWAY?

Mo Better Blues, the title of Spike Lee's fourth feature film, instantly draws attention to itself. What exactly is this "Mo' Better" thing? Lee picked up the phrase from Patti Fears, a a friend from his college days in Atlanta. Lee credits Fears with her unique sense of humor for enlightening him to the phrase "Mo' Better." According to Fears, during one of their phone conversations in the latter 1980s, she told him that it was a slang term she had coined for love making. The colorful phrase stuck with Lee and years later he put it to use when unable to secure permission to use his first choice for a film title.

A LOVE SUPREME WAS THE ORIGINAL TITLE

Initially Lee wanted to use the title from a 1964 album by jazz artist John Coltrane, "A Love Supreme," as the recording inspired him to write a script about a jazz musician whose love for his music affects his relationships. The script was sent to John Coltrane's widow Alice for approval, since she controlled the rights to the title. After reading the story, Alice Coltrane refused to give Lee permission for use of the title as she objected to the profanity and the sexual content of the screenplay. As a comprise she did allow Lee to use a photograph of the "Love Supreme" album cover and a cut from the actual jazz recording in his film.

NOT A LOVE STORY

Having grown up in a household with a father who was a jazz bassist, Lee longed to turn his appreciation for jazz music into a film. In *Mo' Better Blues* he did just that and more by constructing a story about a young trumpet player, "Bleek Gilliam" (Denzel Washington) and the two women, "Indigo Downes" (Joie Lee) and "Clarke Bentancourt" (Cynda Williams), who compete with Bleek's musical career and each other for his affection. Lee did not view his film as a love story, but more of a look at a dedicated musician and his relationships with others including his father "Big Stop" (Dick Anthony Williams), his manager "Giant" (Spike Lee), and his band "The Bleek Gilliam Quintet".

The decision by Lee to make the film was also motivated by what he considered to be inferior films about jazz like *Bird* and *'Round Midnight,* which in his opinion did not do justice to the subject matter. Lee also heard that director Woody Allen was considering a project about jazz as well, which prompted Lee to quickly develop his own script before Allen did. Like many of his other screenplays, Lee generated a first draft of the story in a two week period.

WASHINGTON JOINS THE LEE ENSEMBLE

Denzel Washington, as jazz trumpeter Bleek Gilliam, was key to the casting of the film as the director wanted a romantic lead that appealed to women. The remainder of the characters were cast from Lee's budding ensemble company of actors from his previous films. Bill Nunn and Giancarlo Esposito, who had been with Lee since *School Daze,* portrayed "Bottom Hammer" and "Left Hand Lacey," respectively, musicians in "The Bleek Gilliam Quintet." Joie Lee, Spike's sister, returned for her fourth appearance as "Indigo Downes," one of the two women vying for Bleek's attention. For comedian Robin Harris, who died before the film was released, *Mo'Better* marked his second job with Lee. Harris' first was in *Do The Right Thing,* as "Sweet Dick Willie." In *Mo' Better* he portrayed the jazz club comedian "Butterbean Jones."

For his third, consecutive appearance in a Lee film, actor Samuel Jackson had a small, but pivotal role as a thug. Jackson's voice can also be heard as "Mr. Senor Love Daddy," the radio D.J. from *Do The Right Thing,* during a sequence featuring Jackson and Lee. John Turturro, who played an Italian-American in *Right Thing,* was cast as, "Moe Flatbush," one of the Jewish owners of the jazz club called "Beneath the Underdog" (Lee got the title from the autobiography of jazz composer Charles Mingus). Actor/comedian Steve White, who portrayed "Ahmad" in *Right Thing,* returned this time as a club doorman. Rounding out the ensemble was the director himself, Spike Lee as "Giant," Bleek's unreliable manager.

Of note, a few actors from Lee's first film *She's Gotta Have It* were given small parts in *Mo' Better*. Raye Dowell, who appeared as "Opal Gilstrap" in the first film, was cast as Bleek's friend, Rita, in a brief, non-speaking cameo role. Two other performers, John Canada Terrell and Tracy Camila Johns, who were lovers in Lee's first film, were club patrons in *Mo' Better*.

The other primary members of the cast had never appeared in any of Lee's films before. Actress Cynda Williams made her feature film debut as Bleek's "other woman," "Clarke Bentancourt." Newcomers Jeff Watts as "Rhythm Jones" and Wesley Snipes as "Shadow Henderson" were cast as members of Bleek's Quintet. As Bleek's father "Big Stop," veteran character actor Dick Anthony Williams stepped in on short notice when Lee's first choice, Ossie Davis, became unavailable. John Turturro's brother, Nicholas was selected to play his on-screen brother and club co-owner "Josh Flatbush." Lee completed the cast with his selection of musician/actor Ruben Blades as "Petey," the no-nonsense, neighborhood gambling bookie.

MO' BETTER BUDGET

Universal granted Lee his largest budget to that date, $10 million. The $10 million figure, while being about one million less than what Lee wanted, did permit the construction of an elaborate, two-story jazz club "Beneath the Underdog", designed by Wynn Thomas. The large set made it possible for Lee and his cinematographer, Ernest Dickerson, to use a crane for high angles and sweeping, lyrical shots during the musical numbers inside the club. With the sets in place and the actors well rehearsed, shooting commenced in September of 1989 in and around the New York City area and was completed by the beginning of December of that same year.

Upon its release during the beginning of August of 1990, in about 500 theaters, *Mo' Better Blues* became yet another hit for Lee, and the most successful film featuring jazz to date, with an eventual box office gross of about $18 million.

LEE GETS *FEVER* FOR NEXT FILM

Mo' Better Blues, like all of Lee's films, did not escape without a bit of controversy. The director was criticized for his portrayal of the crooked Jewish club owners, Moe and Joe Flatbush. Lee believed the media was applying a double standard to his work. He found that many reviewers used *Mo' Better* as an opportunity to bring up the issue of stereotypes, while virtually ignoring the subject prior to his film's release.

Critics wouldn't have to wait long to find fault with the content of Lee's work again as his next project would mark a return to large scale controversy. It featured the explosive subject of interracial romance in a script entitled *Jungle Fever.*

Note to the reader: For a full account on the making of *Mo' Better Blues,* I recommend that you read Spike Lee's book of the same title by Spike Lee with Lisa Jones, published by Simon and Schuster, 1990.

9 To Sleep With Anger

Charles Burnett: Writer/Director

(Samuel Goldywn, 1990)

A DEBUT 20 YEARS IN THE MAKING

At the age of 46 Charles Burnett became the oldest director of the initial New Jack filmmakers to make his major motion picture debut. The release of his drama *To Sleep With Anger* starring Danny Glover in the fall of 1990 was Burnett's first feature length film to be distributed on a wide basis. Burnett got the title of his film from an old saying, "Never go to bed angry." The meaning of that phrase becomes evident in the film as a family practically breaks apart during the visit of a mysterious old friend, played by Danny Glover, who gradually disrupts their lives.

Burnett was no newcomer to the world of filmmaking. His first feature length film entitled *My Brother's Wedding* was completed in 1984 on a low-budget of less than $100,000, but the film received little attention at the time. This film was just one of many personal projects that Burnett would struggle to make over the course of almost 20 years as an independent writer/director. Like many of the directors who exhibited a New Jack spirit when it came to filmmaking, Charles Burnett had something to say to his audience. However, he differed from many of the younger directors in that he did not actively seek to make his films within the commercially minded, profit-driven Hollywood system. This difference is perhaps due to the fact that Burnett is clearly from a different generation. His experience as a filmmaker, like that of others, began in film school, but Burnett's education in cinema developed during a turbulent period in U.S. history.

THE 1960s INFLUENCED HIS FILMS

During the late 1960s Burnett attended Los Angeles City College where he pursued a degree in electronics. While at the College, he developed an interest in writing and decided to drop electronics in favor of enrolling as a film student at the University of Southern California at Los Angeles (UCLA). While at UCLA, Burnett learned his craft in an environment that frowned upon commercially-minded, Hollywood style films.

Upon graduation, he made several short films which reflected an almost documentary-like examination of life among different classes of African Americans. In 1977 he both wrote and directed a short black and white drama called *Killer of Sheep* for $10,000. The film was a docu-drama style portrait of a group of African Americans, featuring a down and out man who worked in a sheep slaughterhouse. It would go on to win both the first prize at the U.S. Film Festival as well as the Critics Prize at the Berlin Film Festival in 1981. Ten years later, *Killer of Sheep* would become a part of the prestigious National Film Registry at the Library of Congress. Burnett's film, along with almost 100 other works, was chosen as an important motion picture deemed worthy of preservation due to its cultural and historical significance. His film was also the only film by an African American to be included in the collection.

HALF A MILLION DOLLARS — WITH NO STRINGS ATTACHED

Despite the early success of *Killer of Sheep,* Burnett would continue to struggle financially in an effort to make other films. That problem was eased a bit in 1988 when he received a $275,000 MacArthur Foundation Fellowship. The fellowship, commonly known as the "genius grant," was routinely awarded each year to artists, often at the top of their field. The grant of half a million dollars came with "no strings attached" as the recipient was free to use the money in any way. Burnett used the cash primarily to support himself while he pursued his film career full-time without the burden of holding down a 9 to 5 job. The MacArthur Foundation Fellowship was just one of several prestigious grants Burnett received over the years. Among the other financial gifts were a Guggenheim Foundation Fellowship in 1981, a grant from the National Endowment for the Arts in 1985, and a 1988 Rockefeller Foundation Fellowship.

While Charles Burnett had received ample recognition from the artistic community for his film work by winning festivals, grants, and other awards, it wasn't until the 1990 release of *To Sleep With Anger* that he became known to a larger movie-going audience.

SUPPORT FROM DANNY GLOVER

To Sleep With Anger was destined to be produced, like Burnett's other films, through funding from grants and other philanthropic sources. He was prepared to direct the film with help from the Corporation for Public Broadcasting (CPB), but soon found a dislike for their influence in the project. The deal eventually fell apart as CPB withdrew their offer.

Independent producer Caldecott Chubb, impressed with Burnett's early films, viewed the script for *To Sleep With Anger* as a prime opportunity to work with the director. In 1988 Chubb, who was an executive with a production company called the Edward R. Pressman Film Corporation, brought Burnett's screenplay to the attention of his boss, producer Edward R. Pressman. Pressman was known in the film industry as a veteran producer willing to take the risk of developing new filmmakers. True to his reputation, Pressman agreed to produce Burnett's film and went about raising money for the project.

Attracting additional financing became easier after popular film star Danny Glover became interested. Glover accepted one of the lead acting roles and even became one of the executive producers after contributing money to the film.

With a small budget of just under two million dollars, production started during the spring of 1989 in South Central, Los Angeles, an area Burnett grew up in. Filming was completed within a month as budget constraints forced Burnett to shoot quickly and efficiently, a method that he was well versed with as an independent director.

ANGER FAILS TO ATTRACT AN AUDIENCE

Upon its completion, *To Sleep With Anger* was shown at the 1990 Cannes Film Festival and received favorable response from the international audience in attendance. The Samuel Goldwyn Company was chosen as the film's distributor and a U.S. release was scheduled for the fall of 1990.

Unfortunately, *Anger* vanished quickly from theaters as moviegoers did not turn out to see the film. Director Charles Burnett later blamed Samuel Goldwyn's poor marketing of his film as the primary reason why it failed to garner a larger audience, particularly in black communities. Goldwyn admitted that it had little money to spend on the advertising and marketing of *To Sleep With Anger,* a film many agreed merited better handling.

PART TWO:

The Renaissance Year (1991)

10

New Jack City

Mario Van Peebles: Director/Actor

(Warner Bros., 1991)

A VIOLENT OPENING WEEKEND

On March 8, 1991 the first film of the "Black Film Renaissance," as the year was dubbed by the Hudlin Brothers and their Black Filmmaker Foundation, opened to theaters across the country. It was called *New Jack City*. The film was directed by a rising star in the film industry, 33 year old Mario Van Peebles. Van Peebles' *New Jack City* was a modern gangster story of sorts because it depicted the rise and fall of a fictional New York City drug kingpin named "Nino Brown." The movie instantly exploded at the box office both in terms of financial success and outbreaks of violence at several theaters.

New Jack City earned $7 million during its first weekend making it the number two film at the box office, just behind *Silence of the Lambs*. Due to the fact that *New Jack* was initially distributed on a limited basis, in only 862 theaters across the country, tickets for the film quickly sold out at several movie theaters during the opening weekend. At one Westwood Los Angeles theater approximately 1500 people, after waiting in long lines, were asked to leave because the seats had been oversold. Several people in the crowd became unruly and fights ensued which resulted in almost two hours of rioting and looting. One fatality in New York was linked to the film because a Brooklyn teenager was shot and killed outside a theater showing the movie.

The producers of the film, Doug McHenry and George Jackson, along with director Mario Van Peebles released a written statement to the press expressing their concerns over the weekend of violence. The three men also pointed out that the unfortunate events associated with the film's release were contrary to the anti-drug message of their movie. Warner Bros., the studio that released the film, also issued a press release condemning the violence. The studio later provided additional prints of the film to theaters that were overbooked in addition to security guards.

HE FOLLOWED IN HIS FATHER'S FOOTSTEPS

Director Mario Van Peebles was no stranger to controversy when it came to movies because 20 years earlier his father Melvin Van Peebles had directed an independent film entitled, *Sweet Sweetback's Baadasssss Song* (1971). The film caused an uproar for its portrayal of a black man who murders two racist white police officers and later escapes to Mexico. *Sweetback* went on to become one of the top grossing independent films of all time and served as the catalyst for a wave of black action films in the 1970s. Many of those action films directed primarily by white directors were given the name "Blaxploitation," as they featured not only the cheap thrills of most action-oriented, exploitation films, but concentrated on themes of crime and drugs in the black community. Roughly 20 years later, many feared that a second wave of Blaxploitation movies would result after the enormous success of *New Jack City*.

MARIO'S EARLY START AS AN ACTOR

Despite the unfortunate incidents linked to his film, director Mario Van Peebles was proud of his directorial debut. Although he had worked hard in the industry to become a director, Van Peebles began his movie career as an actor. At the age of 13 he appeared in his father's hit film *Sweet Sweetback's Baadasssss Song*.

After graduating from Columbia University with a degree in economics, Van Peebles got a job as a budget analyst in New York City. He returned to the entertainment industry after quitting his job, became a model, and took acting classes whenever possible. Movie roles soon followed as he was featured in a number of movies including *The Cotton Club, Heartbreak Ridge,* and *Jaws: The Revenge*. Van Peebles went on to become the first black actor to be featured as a lawyer on the NBC show *L.A. Law*.

"SONNY SPOON" BECOMES A DIRECTOR

It was on another NBC show that Van Peebles got his big break as a director. He starred in his own 1988 series Sonny Spoon as a detective who used a variety of accents and disguises to solve cases. The show's producer Stephen J. Cannell gave Van Peebles a chance to direct an episode of *Sonny Spoon*, followed by directing jobs on several of his other TV projects including *21 Jump Street, Wiseguy*, and *Booker*. With previous experience directing theater and music videos, coupled with additional directing jobs in television, Van Peebles quickly gained a reputation as a disciplined director.

VAN PEEBLES GETS NEW JACK DIRECTING JOB

Previous experience as an actor and director worked in Van Peebles favor when producers Doug McHenry and George Jackson selected him to direct *New Jack City*. McHenry and Jackson believed the young director was ideally suited to helm their project after he suggested that the role of a police officer be expanded to add balance to the script, which featured a drug dealer in a lead role. Director Van Peebles even brought his own experience with drug users to the script, having worked in a drug treatment center earlier in his career. He added a scene in which a character named "Pookie" seeks rehabilitation.

Van Peebles' experience of working quickly as a TV director came in handy when he was asked to shoot *New Jack City* on a schedule of 36 days, which was almost half the time afforded to most feature films.

THE "NEW JACK" ORIGINATOR

Around 1988 Warner Bros. had a script about a real life 1970s gangster from Harlem named Leroy "Nicky" Barnes. The screenplay was updated for the 1990s using fictional characters written by journalist Barry Michael Cooper. Cooper was credited with coming up with the phrase "New Jack" in an article he wrote about new trends in music and street culture during the 1980s. According to Cooper, New Jack referred to the influence of street culture on music. Cooper would later apply the New Jack attitude to the characters in his screenplay for *New Jack City*.

A DIVERSE GROUP OF ACTORS IS PICKED

The lead role of the powerful drug dealer "Nino Brown" was reportedly written specifically for actor Wesley Snipes. Director Van Peebles cast rapper Ice-T as the "New Jack" police officer "Scotty Appleton" after overhearing the performer's conversation in a men's room. According to Van Peebles, once he heard Ice-T's tough intonation he wanted to meet the man who sounded right for the role of an undercover police officer. Van Peebles completed his principle casting by adding a performer who was a fellow acting student from years past in New York, Judd Nelson, as the Ice-T's partner "Nick Peretti." Van Peebles even cast himself in the film as "Detective Stone," the man in charge of the undercover operation against drug kingpin Nino Brown.

ADVANCED MARKETING EQUALS BIG BOX OFFICE

New Jack City quickly became the first hit of the Black Film Renaissance of 1991 by earning a total of over $47 million with an original budget of $8.5 million. The success of the movie could be attributed, in part, to the savvy marketing by Warner Brothers. The studio began to promote the film weeks prior to its release. Audience awareness for the project was generated primarily through the music featured on the movie's soundtrack. The soundtrack album featured a line-up of some of the hottest recording talent at that time, including rappers Ice-T and Queen Latifah, along with R & B performers Keith Sweat, Johnny Gill, Teddy Riley with Guy, and Christopher Williams.

FATHER & SON PRODUCE PROJECTS TOGETHER

Van Peebles followed the success of his directorial debut by working on a number of projects both in front and behind the camera. As an actor, he appeared in several TV movies for NBC. A movie he worked on with his father in the late 1980s called *Identity Crisis* was finally released directly to home video and in the form of a behind-the-scenes book. The elder Van Peebles directed the film from a script written by and starring his son as a rapper whose body becomes inhabited by a homosexual fashion designer.

VAN PEEBLES HEADS POSSE

Despite the success of *New Jack City*, Van Peebles found difficulty launching his next project. The studios were eager for him to direct another urban crime drama, but Van Peebles was interested in pursuing other stories about African Americans. By 1992 he was able to convince a British company to give him $9 million, roughly the same budget he had on *New Jack City*, to shoot a western called *Posse*.

Set in Texas of the 1890s, the movie starred Van Peebles as an army deserter from the Spanish-American War. Van Peebles' charater travels to a small town with his "Posse" of fellow deserters, including

Tiny Lister (the body builder featured in *Talkin' Dirty After Dark*), rapper Tone-Loc, and director Charles Lane (*True Identity*, 1991). Actor Blair Underwood was selected to play the town sheriff who clashes with Van Peebles and competes for the affections of a young lady.

Given that Van Peebles wanted to show moviegoers that the old west of hundred years ago was multi-racial, he made a conscious effort to select a multi-ethnic the cast. *Posse* also featured other notable black actors and performers both young and old including Pam Grier (a black-action film star of the 1970s), rapper Big Daddy Kane and the elder filmmaker and Mario's father, Melvin Van Peebles.

Posse made $5 million in its first weekend in theaters. The film, while not a big hit like *New Jack City*, went on to become a modest success at the box office. With two films to his credit Mario Van Peebles was set to continue his track record by developing additional films about the African American experience in America.

II The Five Heartbeats

Robert Townsend: Executive Producer/Co-Writer/Director/Actor

(20th Century Fox, 1991)

THE THREE YEAR WAIT

Moviegoers eager to see director Robert Townsend's next film, after the success of both *Hollywood Shuffle* and Eddie Murphy: Raw, had to wait three years. Townsend was determined to take his time in an effort to create a quality motion picture. He co-wrote a comedy with Keenan Ivory Wayans about a singing group and set out to conduct research by touring with veteran R & B group, "The Dells." During his time on the road with The Dells, Townsend soon discovered the ups and downs of the music industry. As he re-wrote his script, The Dells became the inspiration for a bittersweet, fictional story of the rise and fall of a 1960s vocal group called *The Five Heartbeats*. The Dells also served as the singing voices for the Heartbeats and Townsend had the actors lip-sync to songs performed by the group.

THE SEARCH FOR THE FIVE HEARTBEATS

Townsend scheduled "open casting calls" (where anyone can audition) in Chicago, Los Angeles and New York to provide an opportunity for large numbers of actors and would-be actors to audition for parts in his film. Each actor was videotaped, which was quite a task as several thousand people turned out to audition for the parts. For the major roles in the film, Townsend personally oversaw the casting because he had a very strong sense of what each of the men who would play the Heartbeats would be like as performers. The director found his five Heartbeats in different parts of the country. Michael Wright, an actor from New York, was cast as the leader of the group, "Eddie." A man known simply by a single name Leon, who was featured in Madonna's "Like a Prayer" video as a Saint, was tapped to play "J.T.," a ladies man and the brother to Robert Townsend's character "Duck," the songwriter. To portray the family man of the group, Townsend selected former Chicago school teacher turned actor, Harry J. Lennix. The final Heartbeat was a young actor originally from Washington, D.C., Tico Wells, who had a recurring role on the television program *The Cosby Show*. Wells was chosen to portray "Choirboy," a singer who leaves the security of his church to pursue a career with the Heartbeats.

Although relatively new actors were cast as the Five Heartbeats, Townsend also created cameo roles for several veteran performers. One was a member of the legendary dancing team, "The Nicholas Brothers," Harold Nicholas, as the choreographer "Sarge Johnson" who teaches the Heartbeats a few fancy moves. Diahann Carroll, who in 1969 became the first black actress to have her own television show called *Julia,* was cast as "Eleanor Potter," the wife of the Heartbeats' manager.

TOWNSEND HIRES LEE'S USUAL CREW

With a $10 million budget Townsend shot his film on location in and around Southern California. He chose several people associated with Spike Lee's films to work as crew members on his project. Among them was costume designer Ruthe Carter, who has worked on all of Lee's films. Carter used a variety of clothes which paralleled the rise of the Five Heartbeats from the 1960s to the present day. Another veteran of Lee's movies, production designer Wynn Thomas, provided director Townsend with designs for over 70 locations.

A DISMAL OPENING WEEKEND

After several positive preview screenings with moviegoers, *The Five Heartbeats* opened on March 29, 1991. During its first weekend in the theaters the film made only $1.6 million. As a result, the studio began to quickly curtail its marketing and advertising support of the movie in an effort to cut losses. By the end of its theatrical run Townsend's film barely earned back the cost of its original budget of $10 million. Many analysts blamed the box office failure of the film on a poor marketing campaign. Despite the initial favorable test screenings, audiences simply did not turn out to see the film.

AFTER *HEARTBEATS* TOWNSEND KEEPS BUSY

After the release of *The Five Heartbeats* Robert Townsend went on a short tour featuring some of the performers from the film including The Dells and teenager Tressa Thomas who played Townsend's sister in the movie. Thomas also sang one of the hit songs from the film, "We Haven't Finished Yet."

Seeking a place to house his production company, Townsend converted a small warehouse in Hollywood into what he called "Tinsel Townsend" which not only included offices, but editing equipment and a stage for use by others in the community.

The busy director also became a family man when he and his wife, real estate agent Cheri Jones, had their first child, a girl.

In 1992 Townsend began work on his third original project as a writer/director called *The Meteor Man*. In the film, Townsend played a school teacher who develops superhuman powers after being hit by a meteor.

12 A Rage in Harlem

Bill Duke: Director

(Miramax Films, 1991)

FROM MOVIE ACTOR TO TV DIRECTOR

In 1991 *A Rage In Harlem* may have been 47 year old Bill Duke's feature film directorial debut, but he had over 20 years of experience both as an actor and as a TV director. In his movie roles Duke usually played bad guys like the pimp in *American Gigolo* and a hitman in *Bird On A Wire.* When he wasn't on screen, Duke was usually working behind the camera as a director of episodic television programs like *Hill Street Blues, Miami Vice,* and *Dallas,* just to name a few. Duke directed a feature length movie for public television in 1984 called *The Killing Floor* which dealt with black slaughterhouse workers in Chicago and their efforts to form a union after World War I. He also directed the public television adaption on the play, *A Raisin In The Sun,* starring Danny Glover.

PRODUCERS OF RAGE PICK DUKE AS DIRECTOR

When it came time to select a director for the film adaptation of African-American novelist Chester Himes' novel, *A Rage In Harlem,* producers Stephen Woolley and Kerry Boyle along with their co-producer and lead actor, Forest Whitaker, searched specifically for a black director to bring the work of Himes to the screen. This would be the third time that a book by Himes would become a movie. One of the adaptations, *Cotton Comes To Harlem,* was directed by African American actor Ossie Davis in the 1970s. For the *Rage In Harlem* adaptation the producers wanted someone who had both the cultural background and filmmaking experience necessary to visually translate Himes' depiction of Harlem. Bill Duke was their choice due to his maturity as a filmmaker and his directing background with shows like *Hill Street Blues,* which had a blend of violence and humor much like the Himes novel.

In the screen version of *A Rage In Harlem,* a sultry Southern woman "Imabelle" arrives in Harlem with a trunk of gold. She meets an innocent undertaker "Jackson" and seduces him in order to find a safe hiding place for the gold, because her mean former lover "Slim" has arrived in town looking for the trunk.

HARLEM BASED FILM SHOT IN CINCINNATI

With the selection of Duke as the director, and actor Forest Whitaker already chosen to play one of the leading men, Miramax Films and Palace Productions put together a $9 million budget. Miramax also served as the distributor for the project. Despite the fact that most of the story took place in Harlem, New York, the filmmakers decided to shoot on location in Cincinnati, Ohio. Cincinnati offered the same 1950s style architecture that New York did, but at a lower price.

DUKE AUDITIONS HUNDREDS FOR LEAD ACTRESS

The selection of an actress to play the intelligent, sexy female lead Imabelle was not an easy decision for Duke. He initially auditioned over 300 actresses for the role and later cut the list down to four finalists. Of the four, Duke picked Robin Givens, an actress known primarily for her work on the television show *Head of the Class,* and also as the ex-wife of former heavyweight boxing champ, Mike Tyson. Duke was aware of Givens' highly publicized marital problems with Tyson, and the negative press she received as a result. He put those concerns aside and, based upon Givens' strong screen test, he decided that she was right for the role.

The remainder of the cast consisted of Forest Whitaker as the virginal undertaker "Jackson." Gregory Hines portrayed Whitaker's scheming, con-artist brother "Goldy." Actor Badja Djola was cast as "Slim," Imabelle's lover and partner in crime. Danny Glover completed the primary cast as Harlem gangster "Easy Money."

RAGE TRAILER RECEIVES RESTRICTIVE RATING

On April 4, 1991 a month before *A Rage In Harlem* was scheduled to open in theaters, the Motion Picture Association of America (MPAA) placed a severe rating on the theatrical trailer for the film. The prerelease trailer received an MPAA "red-band" ruling which would only allow it to be shown with "R" or "NC-17" rated films. This ruling would then prevent the trailer from being seen by a wide audience, as the "R" rating restricted children under the age of 17 unless they were accompanied by a parent or guardian, and the "NC-17" barred all children under 17.

The MPAA made its decision based upon a scene in the trailer in which the character played by Gregory Hines pulls out a gun hidden inside a hollowed-out Bible and points it at another person. According to the MPAA's rules, the pointing of a gun at a victim's head required a restrictive rating.

The distributor of *Rage,* Miramax Films, appealed the rating because they argued that the scene involving a gun was meant to be humorous. Miramax's appeal was denied and they quickly re-edited the trailer so that it could be seen with films with less restrictive ratings.

A SLOW START AT THE BOX OFFICE

A Rage In Harlem, which opened in only 500 theaters on May 8, 1991, got off to a slow start. It earned only $2.5 million during its first weekend in release. By the second weekend, *Rage* dropped to $1.4 million.

Despite its dismal financial performance, *Rage* received a number of favorable reviews overall, with Robin Givens and Bill Duke being cited for their impressive debuts as the lead actress and the director, respectively. Robin Givens went on to be cast alongside Eddie Murphy in a big-budget film by New Jack director Reginald Hudlin called *Boomerang.* Bill Duke was subsequently signed by the company New Line Cinema to direct a police thriller called *Deep Cover.*

13 Straight Out of Brooklyn

Matty Rich: Writer/Director

(Samuel Goldwyn, 1991)

A TROUBLED CHILDHOOD

He was born on November 26, 1971, in Brooklyn New York as Matthew Satisfield Richardson. He would later shorten the name to Matty Rich because he didn't think he looked like a "Matthew Richardson." Rich grew up in Brooklyn's poverty stricken Red Hook area in the very same housing projects depicted in his movie *Straight Out of Brooklyn*. In the film a young man resorts to crime in an effort to escape his life of poverty.

Much like the dysfunctional family portrayed in his film, Rich had a father who drank heavily and took out his frustrations on his wife Beatrice in the form of verbal abuse. When Rich was about seven years old he witnessed his father being handcuffed and taken away from their home after an argument with his mother.

Several years later Mrs. Richardson moved her children from the troubled, crime-ridden projects of Red Hook to the safer neighborhood of Park Slope, New York. Rich missed his old friends, so he often went back to visit Red Hook. Mrs. Richardson soon discovered that her son had internalized much of the pain he experienced in his old neighborhood. He often expressed his frustrations to her, being unable to do anything about the condition of his community. His anger was fueled by the fact that by the time he was 13 six of his friends were dead, including his best friend Lamont Logan. The untimely death of Lamont, coupled with the tragic loss of several other friends as well as his aunt and uncle, served as a painful reservoir of experience that Rich would later draw from in the creation of his film.

HE READ 250 BOOKS ABOUT FILMMAKING

Rich's mother suggested he turn his rage and frustration into something that was useful and productive. Since he often watched The

Brady Bunch, Rich wanted to learn more about how he could put his experiences, which he found to be far different than the families on television, onto the screen. To that end Mrs. Richardson gave her 10 year Matty his first film book, which soon caused him to foster an immense hunger to learn as much as he could about the craft. Rich says that he had read approximately 250 books about filmmaking by the time he was 17.

THREE WEEK'S AT NYU

After a year long stint in New York's John Jay College of Criminal Justice, where he had entertained thoughts of pursuing a career in law, Rich left the school to concentrate on his goal of making a film. In 1988 he resumed his education by attending a summer film program at New York University's School of Continuing Education for three weeks. After learning how to fashion his story into a script, Matty did not accept NYU's invitation to enroll full-time. Instead, he went about writing a screenplay called *Straight Out of Brooklyn.*

THE REHEARSALS BEGIN

Rich placed an ad in the trade publication *Backstage* calling for actors to perform in his film. Many of the 2,000 people that turned out for the casting call didn't take him seriously, but a few willing actors did, and they were chosen for his film. The group of actors was determined to stay with their young director because he gave them the impression that he actually had the money to shoot a movie.

While rehearsing the cast for six months in his home, Rich struggled to come up with the necessary financing for his project. Realizing that he did not have enough money to begin shooting, one of the actresses, Dorise Black, put Rich together with her husband Allen. Allen Black had both a background in business and a keen interest in filmmaking, just the combination Rich needed to get his project off the ground.

THE FUNDRAISING TAKES OFF

Black and Rich quickly went to work on a plan to finance the film. The initial start-up capital came from Rich as he managed to raise about $12,000 from the credit cards of family members. The cards provided just enough money to shoot roughly 15 minutes of 35mm film. Black suggested cutting the footage into a trailer in an effort to attract investors to the project. Next, Rich went to a New York radio station WLIB and convinced disk jockey Mark Riley to give him one hour of time to address the station's predominantly black audience. During that hour on the radio Rich spoke passionately about the opportunity to create a film with money from African Americans. Listeners willing to invest in the project were invited to a screening of the trailer.

At the initial screening a number of people came forward and donated a total of $40,000. Rich then presented additional screenings with new trailers, which resulted in a grand total of about $77,000.

A POWERFUL NEW FRIEND

While editing portions of his work at a Manhattan post-production facility, Rich had a chance meeting with film director Jonathan Demme. Demme was in the same building as Rich because he was editing a film called *The Silence of the Lambs*, a movie that would later go on to sweep the 1991 Academy Awards including Best Picture and Best Director for Demme. After stopping by to see what the young filmmaker was working on, Demme began to visit Rich's editing sessions on a regular basis. He quickly helped Matty find the necessary funding to complete his film by introducing him to an independent film production firm, The Deutchman Company. Deutchman was able to garner completion funding from American Playhouse Theatrical Films, after Playhouse's executive producer Lindsay Law saw a rough cut of *Straight Out of Brooklyn.* Law provided roughly $260,000 for post-production and a deal to air Rich's film as part of the PBS series *American Playhouse* during January of 1993.

THE PUBLICITY TOUR

Straight Out of Brooklyn went on to win a Special Jury Award at the 1991 Sundance Film Festival, a yearly event held in Utah, founded by actor Robert Redford. The festival proved to be ideal for Rich as critics and filmmakers began to generate a positive response to his film, thus providing a much needed launch for the low budget feature.

After the Sundance festival the film's distributor, The Samuel Goldwyn Company, released Rich's film during the summer of 1991 in a few cities at a time to build audience word-of-mouth. In an effort to further promote his movie, Rich went on a publicity tour and even made an appearance on the popular late-night program of

The Arsenio Hall Show. He also had the opportunity to speak to his peers about his film as he visited high schools across the country.

Straight Out of Brooklyn would go on to gross about $2.7 million by the end of 1991. Considering its original cost of just $260,000, the film was viewed as a successful low-budget production.

REACHING BACK TO HIS COMMUNITY

Rich quickly established himself as an entrepreneur after the release of his film. He formed a production company called *Blacks N' Progress,* major studies pursued him, and he became a staff director with *The Directors' Chair,* a TV commercial company. Rich also didn't wait very long to share his success with the people of his hometown. He opened a clothing store in Brooklyn during the summer of 1991 called *"Matty Rich's Red Hook."* The store's merchandise was primarily for high school/college shoppers with many of the items offered at discount rates. The store also featured Rich's own clothing line called *Matty Rich Wear.*

It would be almost two years until Matty Rich would begin work on his second project. The Disney studios hired Rich to direct a $5 million film called *The Inkwell.* Released in 1994, *The Inkwell* dealt with African American youth growing up in the 1970s.

14

Jungle Fever

Spike Lee: Writer/Producer/Director/Actor

(Universal, 1991)

A RETURN TO CONTROVERSY

Spike Lee's fifth project in six years, the $14 million *Jungle Fever,* would mark a return to the immense media scrutiny and controversy that usually surrounded his work. The film featured a married black architect from Harlem who has an affair with his white secretary from Bensonhurst New York.

Lee's inspiration for the film was an 1989 incident which took place in Bensonhurst. A black teenager named Yusef Hawkins went to the predominantly white Bensonhurst neighborhood to look at a used car. A group of men believed Hawkins was there to see a white girl they knew, and as a result he was shot. When selecting locations for Fever, Lee made the decision to film scenes in the same neighborhood where Hawkins was killed.

THE LEE ENSEMBLE RETURNS

Many of Lee's collaborators on his previous films returned for *Fever,* including cinematographer Ernest Dickerson, co-producer Monty Ross, line producer Jon Kilik, production designer Wynn Thomas, costume designer Ruth Carter, and casting director Robi Reed.

For the soundtrack music Lee departed from his usual heavy use of jazz scoring for a more contemporary sound featuring 11 new songs by Stevie Wonder. Lee wanted to collaborate with Wonder ever since he wrote one of the songs for Lee's second film, *School Daze* (1988).

As for the casting, Lee selected a diverse group of actors. Wesley Snipes was cast in the lead role as "Flipper Purify" and Lonette McKee as his wife, "Drew." Annabella Sciorra was chosen for the role of Flipper's secretary "Angela Tucci," whom he later has an affair with. Actress Cynda Williams who was in Lee's previous film *Mo' Better*

Blues had a small part as Flipper's initial secretary, but apparently her scenes were cut from the finished film.

Although Lee cast himself in the film as Flipper's friend "Cyrus," he also appeared on an opening message which was edited out of the film. In response to critics of his last film *Mo' Better Blues,* who suggested that Lee presented a stereotyped portrayal of Jews, Lee directly addressed the camera and told them to kiss his "black ass." Universal Studios, the film's production company, asked Lee to remove his opening remarks.

Along with Wesley Snipes, several other actors who worked with Lee in the past were given parts including John Turturro as Angela Tucci's former boyfriend "Paulie." Ossie Davis and his wife Ruby Dee portrayed Flipper's parents, and Samuel Jackson played their drug addicted son "Gator."

DEALING WITH THE DRUG ISSUE

When Lee's film *Do The Right Thing* was released in 1989 some members of the media asked him why he didn't include drugs in the film. Lee was quick to point out that no other director had been asked that question, and secondly, the focus of the film was on race relations, not drugs. With *Jungle Fever* Lee felt the time was right to deal with the issue of drugs, specifically, the epidemic of crack cocaine.

Lee illustrated the destructive nature of crack in several scenes. For a sequence in which the Wesley Snipes character Flipper searches the streets for his crack-addicted brother Gator, Lee heightened the dramatic intensity of the action by using the Stevie Wonder song "Livin' for the City" on the soundtrack. The song is played for its entire length of seven minutes and 23 seconds. The scene culminates when Flipper finds his brother in a huge, smoke-filled crack-house referred to as the "Taj Mahal."

When *Jungle Fever* was shown at the Cannes Film Festival in the spring of 1991, prior to its national release, an international jury selected Samuel L. Jackson as Best Supporting Actor for his portrayal of Gator.

MEDIA GETS HOT OVER *FEVER*

The June 1991 opening of *Jungle Fever* was greeted with great interest by the media. TV talk shows like *The Oprah Winfrey Show* aired programs dealing with the issue of interracial relationships. Magazines featured the topic as well. *Newsweek* magazine featured the stars of the film, Annabella Sciorra and Wesley Snipes, on its June 10, 1991 cover with the headline "Tackling A Taboo: Spike Lee's Take on Interracial Romance."

ANOTHER BOX OFFICE HIT FOR LEE

Each of Spike Lee's films were financially successful and his fifth project *Jungle Fever* was no exception. Made with a budget of $14 million, the movie grossed about $32 million in theaters during 1991.

LEE PREPARES FOR *X*

While promoting *Jungle Fever,* Spike Lee also announced that he was to begin work on the biggest project of his career with Denzel Washington playing the lead character. The film was about the life of the slain religious leader *Malcolm X.*

15 Boyz N The Hood

John Singleton: Writer/Director

(Columbia, 1991)

A RECORD BREAKING DEBUT

On February 19, 1992 John Singleton, then 24 years old, became the youngest filmmaker and the first African American to be nominated in the Best Director category of the Academy Awards for his first feature film *Boyz N The Hood*. The previous record holder was the 26 year old director of *Citizen Kane* (1941), Orson Welles. Despite the success of their respective films, Welles and Singleton did not win the Academy Award.

Singleton was also nominated for Best Original Screenplay and became the second African American to hold that distinction. The first was Spike Lee for his 1989 film *Do The Right Thing*. Neither filmmaker took home the award.

Given that *Boyz N The Hood* told the fictional, yet highly realistic story of three young black men growing up in a troubled South Central Los Angeles neighborhood, Singleton was rather surprised about the nominations. He commented to the press that he really made the film for his peers and clearly didn't expect it to appeal to such a wide audience. That audience translated to a gross of over $58 million in ticket sales during the theatrical release of Boyz, which made it the biggest grossing film by an African American writer/director.

The box office success of Boyz N The Hood, coupled with the double Academy Award nomination, could be seen as quite a surprising achievement given Singleton's age. However, just a few years prior to his historic debut, the young filmmaker had clearly begun to prepare for his career.

GROWING UP IN THE "HOOD"

Like many New Jack directors, John Singleton drew upon experiences from his own life to create a realistic depiction of African

Americans. Singleton was born on January 6, 1968 and grew up in South Central Los Angeles, California, a locale which received world-wide media attention on April 29, 1992. On that day riots erupted in South Central and other parts of Los Angeles after a predominately white jury acquitted four white police officers in the trial of black motorist Rodney King. Prior to the riots, South Central was noted for its gang warfare — an ever present reality which Singleton grew up with.

When he was 12 years old Singleton's parents, Shelia Ward and Danny Singleton, who lived separately, agreed that in order for their son to stay out of trouble, he should live with his mother during the week and with his father on weekends. As John Singleton entered high school he began to spend more time with his father in the suburban community of Inglewood, California.

Singleton has commented that were it not for the strong presence of his father he might have grown up like "Dough Boy," the fatherless character from his film that spends his early life in constant trouble with the law.

INSPIRED BY *STAR WARS* AND SPIKE LEE

The 1977 science-fiction film Star Wars was Singleton's inspiration for pursuing a career in filmmaking. He was only nine years old when he saw the film with his father, but it made such a strong impression on him that he seriously considered a career in the film industry.

His inspiration was bolstered almost a decade later when Singleton went to the Los Angeles premiere of a film called, *She's Gotta Have It* (1986). It was directed by a first-time African American director named Spike Lee. After meeting Lee at the screening, Singleton became even more confident that he too could become a director.

During this time Singleton was also developing a flair for writing as he would often jot down his experiences in journals. By his last year of high school the budding filmmaker decided to fully concentrate on writing, because he was told that screenplays were the backbone of the film industry. After graduating from high school Singleton enrolled in the Filmic Writing Program at the University of South California (USC). While at USC, Singleton was quickly recognized for his talent. He won several top writing honors including the

Robert Riskin Award and two Jack Nicholson Writing Awards for feature-length screenplays.

SINGLETON'S BIG BREAK

Before he even graduated from college, John Singleton was signed to a contract with one of Hollywood's biggest talent firms, Creative Artists Agency (CAA). While serving as a script reader for Columbia Pictures, as part of his senior year internship, Singleton came across many horrible scripts and told his boss about the poor quality. She then read some of John's scripts and passed them along to an agent at CAA and soon the agency offered to sign the young film student to a contract. One of Columbia's vice presidents of production, an African American woman named Stephanie Allain, was largely credited with establishing Singleton at Columbia.

After graduating from USC, Singleton sent his scripts around Hollywood to several producers. TV and music industry producer, Russell Simmons read the screenplay for *Boyz N The Hood* and was so impressed with its quality that he offered to produce it for Columbia Pictures, a studio where he was trying to establish a business relationship. Meanwhile, Singleton's script was already generating interest within the studio and unfortunately for Simmons, Columbia decided to deal directly with Singleton.

HE DEMANDED THE DIRECTOR'S CHAIR

Overnight Singleton became a hot commodity at the studio based upon Russell Simmons extreme interest in his script. Columbia quickly offered to purchase *Boyz N The Hood,* but Singleton was adamant about directing the film. He wanted to preserve his story as crafted in the screenplay. Despite the fact that he had made only a few super-8mm films while in college, Singleton stuck to his guns and won the right to bring his story to the screen. Columbia's Chairman at the time, Frank Price, decided to trust Singleton as a first time director based upon the strength of the screenplay and his strong desire to direct. The studio set a budget of $6 million for the film and also signed Singleton to a lucrative three year contract which allowed him to make as many movies as he wanted during that period.

CASTING YEARS AHEAD OF SHOOTING

Singleton had very little trouble casting two of the major roles since he had written the script with specific people in mind. First, actor Larry Fishburne and second, rap recording star and fellow South Central native Ice Cube, who's given name is O'Shay Jackson. Fishburne had been approached by Singleton when the two first met in 1988 on the set of the CBS children's television program *Pee Wee's Playhouse.* Singleton was working as a production assistant on the show and Fishburne was playing a character named "Cowboy Curtis." Fishburne found that Singleton wanted to hear stories about what it was like to work with Spike Lee (Fishburne had a role in Lee's 1988 film *School Daze).* Singleton told Fishburne that he wanted to direct films someday. Three years later he fulfilled his dream by casting the actor as the father "Furious Styles" in his film.

As for the casting of rap singer Ice Cube, Singleton had him in mind for the role of "Dough Boy" when he wrote the script. In fact, Singleton got the title for his film from a song Ice Cube wrote years earlier, called "Boyz N The Hood," while a member of the rap group N.W.A. (Niggers With Attitude). In 1989 Singleton spoke to Ice Cube at a gathering organized for the Nation of Islam's religious leader Minister Louis Farrakhan. Ice Cube listened to Singleton talk about his script, but reportedly he didn't take Singleton very seriously. However, a few months later the rapper received the script for *Boyz,* was impressed with Singleton's story, and agreed to commit to the project.

SHOOTING ON LOCATION IN SOUTH CENTRAL

On October 1, 1990, just five months after Columbia Pictures received the script for *Boyz,* production began on location in South Central Los Angeles. Several people from the local community also had the opportunity to participate in the film as Singleton often selected extras from the on-lookers who came out to see his movie being filmed in their neighborhood. In an effort to achieve a realistic depiction of life in South Central, warts and all, Singleton consulted with several gang members from the area to aid in the authenticity of the production. The director also wanted to assure them that he was not planning to film a sensationalistic and unrealistic portrayal of gang life.

BOYZ GOES TO CANNES

Boyz N The Hood was invited to the Cannes Film Festival in France during May of 1991 to be screened in the "Un Certain Regard" portion of the festival, outside of the awards competition. Screenings for the film were packed. An international audience of moviegoers, filmmakers, and journalists were clamoring to see *Boyz.* At one packed screening in particular, dozens of people were turned away.

After a wave of positive critical responses to the film at Cannes, *Boyz* was set to premiere in the United States and was praised by the media and others in the industry for its anti-violence message.

VIOLENCE AT THE BOX OFFICE

Boyz opened on July 12, 1991 in 837 theaters and grossed $10 million in its first three days, placing it as the number three film at the box office that weekend, just behind *Terminator 2* and *101 Dalmatians.* Unfortunately, violence broke out at a few theaters. Over 30 people were injured and three died as a result of the violence.

Singleton visited several theaters in L.A. on the film's opening night and saw firsthand what caused some of the violence. At one theater where a disturbance took place, the seats were oversold. The theater management reportedly also neglected to inform the young ticket holders why they were being asked to leave the theater.

THE MOST PROFITABLE FILM OF 1991

After the initial weekend violence, eight theaters pulled *Boyz* from its screens. Singleton and a number of other black filmmakers quickly took to the airwaves to assure moviegoers that the violence was not caused by the movie itself.

Some of the theaters still showing the film increased security and one week after the film opened things began to quickly change. A number of theater owners, clearly motivated by the box office success of the film, asked Columbia Pictures for permission to add the film to their screens. By Friday (July 19, 1992) one week after the film opened, Boyz had increased its distribution from 829 theaters to 920.

Boyz N The Hood went on to gross an estimated $56 million making it the most profitable film of 1991 given its original budget of only $6 million, about one fourth the cost of the average Hollywood film at that time.

A HIT ON HOME VIDEO

The March 1992 home video release of *Boyz* proved to be successful as well. It was the number one video rental for four consecutive weeks. "No more excuses. It's time to see *Boyz N The Hood,"* read the headline from a print ad for the video, which was clearly addressed to moviegoers who avoided seeing the film in theaters.

The beginning of each home video contained a special message from Singleton. He both directed and starred in the public service announcement which appealed for donations to benefit the United Negro College Fund.

JACKSON SELECTS SINGLETON TO DIRECT *TIME*

Pop music superstar Michael Jackson chose Singleton to direct a music video for his song *Remember the Time* from his *Dangerous* album. The film was shot on a sound stage with an elaborate set designed in an ancient Egyptian style. Actor/comedian Eddie Murphy was cast as a King Ramses, fashion model Iman as Queen Nefertiti, and a cameo appearance was made by former basketball star "Magic" Earving Johnson as a royal announcer. The video made its world premiere on the Fox Network to an audience of millions.

THE RIOTS AFFECTED HIS NEXT FILM

On April 29, 1992 Singleton was in route to a location for his second film *Poetic Justice,* a movie about male/female relationships starring recording artist Janet Jackson, when he heard the "not guilty" verdict in the "Rodney King" beating trial. Since he was driving near the site of the trial in Simi Valley, California, Singleton decided to visit the courthouse where the trial had taken place. The director spoke to the news media and commented that the unjust verdict, in his opinion, would light a time bomb in the community. True to his prediction, and that of many others, several parts of Los Angeles went up in flames that day.

After the riots Singleton made plans to incorporate the aftermath into his film *Poetic Justice,* thus becoming the first film after the tragic event to deal with the situation.

16

Talkin' Dirty After Dark

Topper Carew: Writer/Director

(New Line Cinema, 1991)

AN EARLY CAREER IN PUBLIC TELEVISION

Topper Carew made his feature film directorial debut with the 1991 New Line Cinema release *Talkin' Dirty After Dark*, but it was not the start of his career as a filmmaker. Years prior to moving into feature films Carew worked as a producer of educational shows for the Public Broadcasting Service (PBS). While serving as the producer of a 1970s show called *Rebop*, for Boston based PBS station WGBH, Carew developed the concept for a production company called Rainbow TV Works. Like *Rebop*, the mandate of Rainbow TV was to help viewers of different races and cultures to have a mutual respect and understanding for each other. During his ten years as president of the company (1974-1984) Carew was responsible for a number of highly successful educational programs including *The Righteous Apples*.

FROM PUBLIC TV TO FEATURE FILMS

While producing shows for public television, Carew began to develop feature film projects. In 1983 he served as producer of the Universal Studios movie *D.C. Cab* which was set in his hometown, Washington, D.C. The film starred actress/singer Irene Cara and former bouncer turned actor, Mr. T. The low budget project was a modest success for the studio and as a result they pursued a working relationship with Carew.

About one year after the release of *D.C. Cab* Universal entered into a deal with Carew which gave them an exclusive "first-look" at all of his productions, for both television and film, while in their planning stages. With Carew busy developing large scale entertainment projects, his business partner and wife, Alyce took over as president of the Rainbow TV Works.

CAREW GETS *LOOSE* IN SYNDICATION

During the fall of 1987 Topper Carew's company, Golden Groove Productions, in association with MCA and Tribune Entertainment, produced a television show called *Bustin' Loose* which was based upon the 1978 film of the same title by his friend, director Michael Schultz. Carew's TV version retained the plot of the Schultz film, with a social worker played by Vonetta McGee, who cares for a group of unruly children along with a man forced to do community service, Jimmy Walker, after he's is convicted for stealing.

Instead of relying on network television, Carew chose to distribute the show through first-run syndication. Syndication once involved only the selling of older network shows on a city by city basis, but first-run syndication of new programs like Carew's *Bustin' Loose* could now be offered to a wider TV audience. By syndicating the show Carew was able to sell it specifically to cities with large black populations. However, the show did not fare very well in the competitive syndication market and left the air after just one season.

THE MOVE INTO FEATURE FILMS

For his first directing effort Carew wrote a sexually suggestive comedy called *Talkin' Dirty After Dark*. The movie was budgeted at just under $1 million, and it dealt with a group of comedians each vying for the chance to take the stage at a fictional Los Angeles nightclub called "Dukies'." In addition to the action on the stage, many of the comedians pursued love interests behind the scenes. Actor/comedian Martin Lawrence, featured as the D.J. with bad-breath "Bilel" in *House Party* (1990), had the starring role as the ambitious stand-up comedian "Terry." Terry has an affair with the club owner's wife, comedian Jedda Jones, so that she would convince her husband John Witherspoon to give Terry more stage time at the club.

THE RETURN TO TELEVISION

Talkin' Dirty After Dark opened during August of 1991 and quickly vanished from movie theaters. The broad suggestive comedy unfortunately did not catch on with movie audiences. The film grossed $1 million which could be seen as a disappointment given that it cost almost $1 million to produce. Despite the failure of the film, Carew moved on to another project with the film's star, Martin Lawrence.

One year after the release of *Talkin' Dirty After Dark* Carew returned to television as the executive producer of a TV show called *Martin,* starring Martin Lawrence as a radio D.J., for the Fox television network.

During its first season *Martin* was aired on Thursday evenings after the hit animated show *The Simpsons.* In less than one year the show became successful in the TV ratings and a favorite among young audiences, thus providing yet another hit for Topper Carew.

17 True Identity

Charles Lane: Writer/Director/Actor

(Touchstone, 1991)

HE BEGAN MAKING FILMS AS A TEENAGER

Director Charles Lane knew early on what he wanted to do for the rest of his life and that was to make films. He made short movies with Super-8mm equipment while still a teenager during the late 1960s.

He continued to pursue his career goal in college as he enrolled in the film program at the State University of New York at Purchase. The young filmmaker soon became noticed for his work, winning the student Academy Award in 1976 for a short film entitled *A Place In Time.*

Upon graduation from the State University in 1980, Lane found that film production jobs were scarce and trying to develop his own projects was an even greater task. So, to make a living he often worked on scripts written by others, as a "script doctor," using his skills to improve upon their work.

A CHANCE TO DIRECT HIS OWN FILM

A total of 13 years elapsed before Charles Lane would find the funding to direct his own film. In 1989 a friend of Lane's put up the necessary $200,000 for the filmmaker to shoot a 36 minute, black and white film called *Sidewalk Stories*. The film featured Lane as a homeless artist and his two year-old daughter Nicole as an orphan that he cares for. The film was a tribute of sorts to legendary film actor/director Charles Chaplin's comedies.

Lane shot his project on a brisk two week schedule and quickly edited the film so that he could enter it into festivals. That strategy paid off as Lane was able to garner an invitation to screen his movie at the largest international exhibition of work by filmmakers, the Cannes Film Festival in France.

At the 1989 Cannes Festival, Lane won the prestigious "Prix du Publique" (Public Prize) and a distribution deal from Island Pictures, the company that handled director Spike Lee's first film *She's Gotta Have It* (1986). Island put *Sidewalk Stories* in limited release given that it was considered more of a low-budget art film. Despite the fact that many moviegoers never got a chance to see his film, Lane did attract a number of favorable reviews from movie critics.

THE LONG WAIT FOR THE NEXT FILM

Years would pass once again before Lane would direct his next film. In 1991 at the age of 37 he finally made his feature film directorial debut and a bit of history at the same time. Lane was chosen by the Disney studios to be their first African American director with a project called *True Identity* produced through their Touchstone film company. The $16 million film was written by Andy Beckman, based upon a short movie he wrote for Eddie Murphy called *White Like Me* which aired on the television program *Saturday Night Live*. In the movie Murphy had himself made up to appear white so that he could truly study and observe white people.

In the feature film version, aspiring actor "Miles Pope," played by black Englishman and comedian Lenny Henry, on the run from a mob hitman, is disguised as a white man by his friend, a make-up artist, portrayed by Lane. Lane also re-wrote the script for the film to reflect a more truthful representation of black people.

Upon its release during the fall of 1991, *True Identity* performed poorly at the box office. By the end of that year it grossed a total of only $5 million which was tragic as the film was made at a cost of $16 million.

As for director Charles Lane, he continued to develop an original screenplay he wrote called *Skins*. The film was an interracial love story/comedy that Lane wanted to direct as his next project.

Lane also returned to work in front of the camera as an actor when he was given a featured comedic role in director Mario Van Peebles' 1993 western, *Posse*.

18

Livin' Large!

Michael Schultz: Director

(Samuel Goldwyn, 1991)

A VETERAN DIRECTOR

Of the few African American directors working in Hollywood, Michael Schultz has the longest and perhaps the most successful track record with regard to feature films. His career in the movie industry spans 20 years. He became a director near the end of the blaxploitation era of the 1970s and continued with one successful project after another. During the early 1980s Schultz was one of the few active black film directors in Hollywood. After an absence from feature films during the latter 1980s, he returned in 1991 at the age of 52 with a comedy called *Livin' Large!* about a homeboy from Atlanta, "Dexter," who dreams of being an anchorman and one day gets his big chance. Dexter becomes successful after he "sells out" his black community by reporting sensational news stories about friends and family.

HIS BACKGROUND IN THE THEATER

Although Schultz amassed quite a career as a director of movies, he got his start in the theater as a director and one of the founders of the New York based Negro Ensemble. His first big broadway directing job was the play *Does a Tiger Wear a Necktie?*. One of the young stars that he directed in that play, Al Pacino, won a Tony Award for his performance.

As the decade of the 1970s began, Schultz expanded his direction of stage plays to encompass television. In 1971 he served as the director of a PBS adaptation of Lorraine Hansberry's autobiographical play, *To Be Young, Gifted and Black*. Schultz's talent as a TV director was soon recognized when he went on to win a Christopher Award for his direction of an adaptation of playwright Lonne Elder III's work, *Ceremonies in Dark Old Men*.

COOLEY HIGH WAS HIS FIRST HIT

In 1974 after over a decade of work in the theater Schultz made the transition from stage to film directing with the feature film *Cooley High*. Set in 1964, it told a coming of age story about black teens growing up in a tough South Side Chicago neighborhood. The film was based upon the experiences of African American writer Eric Monte. Schultz met with Monte and compiled a number of his funniest stories into a script. *Cooley High* was independently produced with a budget just under $1 million on a quick, 25 day shooting schedule. The movie not only helped to launch the career of young actors like Glynn Turman and Lawrence Hilton Jacobs, but also established Schultz's reputation as a comedy director. This reputation was solidified with the success of his next film *Car Wash* (1976), which starred several popular comedians including George Carlin, Franklyn Ajaye, and Richard Pryor.

BUILDING A TRACK RECORD IN THE 1970s

The highly profitable *Car Wash* lead to a string of films with Richard Pryor which included *Greased Lighting* (1976), *Which Way Is Up?* (1977), and *Bustin' Loose* (1978).

After collaborating with Pryor on several movies, Schultz directed his first feature with a predominantly white cast in 1978, the screen adaptation of the Beatles' *Sgt. Pepper's Lonely Hearts Club Band.* The film served as an acting vehicle for the 1970s disco trio The Bee Gees and featured a new stand-up comedian at the time named Steve Martin.

THE 80s MARK A RETURN TO COMEDIES

In the 1980s Schultz returned to comedies when he directed actor Denzel Washington's film debut *Carbon Copy* (1981), which was about a black man who discovers his white father. Schultz then directed two very successful films in a row, the martial arts/romantic comedy *The Last Dragon* (1985) and the teen musical/drama *Krush Groove* (1985). *Krush Groove* starred a number of black recording artist like Run-DMC and Sheila E., and it was one of the first films to incorporate rap music. The film had a budget of $3 million and grossed over $15 million at the box office.

During the latter 1980s Schultz directed another youth comedy, *Disorderlies* (1987), featuring the slapstick antics of the rap group *The Fat Boys*.

HIS FIRST FILM OF THE 1990s IS LARGE

During the Black Film Renaissance of 1991 Schultz's first film of the 1990s, a comedy called *Livin' Large!* was released. The script for the film, by African American writer William Mosely Payne, came to his attention because his friend and fellow filmmaker, director Topper Carew, suggested that he develop the project. Schultz saw the comedy, about a young man who essentially sells his soul and assimilates into a white environment to become successful, as an opportunity to explore the notion of giving up one's culture in order to make it in America.

With the production company Samuel Goldwyn behind him, providing financing and distribution, Schultz shot the film with a budget of $5.5 million on location in Atlanta, Georgia with the working title, *The Tapes of Dexter Jackson*. The main character "Dexter Jackson," played by newcomer T.C. Carson, uses his VHS camera to practice being a TV reporter. The title of the film was later changed to *Livin' Large!,* which better reflected Dexter's goal to be successful at any cost.

Upon its release in the fall of 1991, the film was met with primarily bad reviews and poor box office attendance. *Livin' Large* had a budget of $5.5 million and grossed about the same amount.

SCHULTZ DEVELOPS MORE FILMS

After the release of *Livin' Large!* Schultz had a schedule-full of projects in various stages of development. As one of the oldest of the New Jack filmmakers, Schultz showed no signs of slowing down.

19 Hangin' With The Homeboys

Joseph B. Vasquez: Writer/Director

(New Line Cinema, 1991)

HALF BLACK/HALF PUERTO RICAN

Twenty-eight year old Joseph B. Vasquez would be the first filmmaker during the Black Film Renaissance of 1991 to cast both blacks and Hispanics in prominent roles for his film *Hangin' With the Homeboys*. This was not surprising since Vasquez himself is racially mixed, being half black and half Hispanic. In his film four men in their 20s, two black and two Hispanic, get together and "hang-out" in the South Bronx. Through a series of misadventures over the course of one night, each man must come to grips with his hopes, fears, and ambitions for the future.

HANGIN' WAS NOT HIS FIRST FEATURE

Vasquez started making movies with a super-8mm camera at the age of 12. As a professional filmmaker he directed two feature films prior to *Hangin'* that did not receive wide distribution. While working as a film editor of movie trailers, for a company called Films Around the World, Vasquez saved about $30,000 to produce and direct his first film called *Street Stories*. His employers were impressed with the film and put up the money to produce another project entitled *The Bronx War*. The $350,000 gang film was released in 1991. It basically bypassed a substantial theatrical release and went straight to home video and cable television.

HOMEBOYS WAS BASED UPON HIS EXPERIENCES

Vasquez wrote the screenplay for *Hangin' With the Homeboys*, which won a screenwriting award at the 1991 Sundance Film Festival, in just three days. He was able to complete the story rather quickly because each of the four characters represented a stage in his life. Two of the characters, "Fernando" (Nestor Serrano) and "Willie" (Doug E. Doug) have identity problems. Fernando, who is Hispanic, pretends that he is Italian and insists that everyone call him Vinnie. Willie, on the other hand, uses his race as an African American for an excuse to explain why he doesn't have a job.

In an encounter with a young black woman at a bar, Willie alleges that she is "perpetrating a fraud" for "hanging out with a white girl." She in turn calls Willie a fraud and proceeds to prove it by asking him if he ever got involved with anything to help black people, or if he even bothered to vote. Willie, realizing that she has uncovered his deception, begins to stutter and is unable to respond.

The two other characters "Johnny" (John Leguizamo) and "Tom" (Mario Joyner) both suffer from poor self-esteem and doubts about their future. Johnny avoids going to college because his friends tell him that it's not necessary. He is prompted to reconsider applying for school after speaking to an attractive college student during his night out. She encourages him to ignore the advice of his friends and give college a try.

Tom, on the other hand, an aspiring actor who boasts that he almost had a part in the film *Rainman,* is unable to find acting work and instead sells magazines over the phone. The only acting opportunities available to Tom are the staged arguments that he and his fellow homeboys perform in public places like the subway.

NEW LINE LOOKS FOR *PARTY* IN *HOMEBOYS*

The distributor of *Hangin' With the Homeboys,* New Line Cinema, according to Vasquez, misunderstood the intended audience for his film. Vasquez wrote a story about young adults, while New Line was hoping to target the mass teen audience in the same way as they did with their 1990 hit *House Party.*

Teenagers were recruited for test screenings of *Hangin'* and the film was met with mixed responses. The teens apparently preferred movies with sex and violence, which *Hangin'* clearly lacked. Vasquez has commented that the test audiences were probably too young to appreciate the mature nature of his film.

New Line scheduled a summer release for *Hangin With the Homeboys* in 1991, but later restricted its opening to only New York theaters. The executives at the company delayed the national release of the film until September because they claimed that moviegoers might have confused their movie title with *Boyz N the Hood* which was released in July of that year.

WAITING FOR THE RIGHT PROJECT

Despite positive reviews and several awards, *Hangin' With Homeboys* had a poor showing at the box office, perhaps due to its scarce marketing campaign and delayed release pattern. New Line produced the film on a budget of $2 million, and it apparently lost money during its theatrical release as it only grossed half a million dollars.

Realizing his apparent talent, studios offered Vasquez a number of screenplays to direct. Vasquez however found many of the scripts to be weak teen comedies or gang films. He instead choose to develop his own scripts in an effort to direct a project he really cared for.

20 House Party 2

George Jackson & Doug McHenry: Directors

(New Line Cinema, 1991)

THE FIRST MOVIE SEQUEL OF THE RENAISSANCE

The 1990 film *House Party* had a budget of $2.5 million and grossed over $27 million, thus making it one of the most profitable films of that year. Like most Hollywood films that performed well at the box office, a sequel was inevitable. The distributor of the first *House Party*, New Line Cinema, was unable to persuade the film's creators, the Hudlin Brothers, to return for the sequel, House Party 2. New Line then turned to another successful African American duo, Doug McHenry and George Jackson. As business partners, McHenry and Jackson served as producers of a string of movie hits including *Krush Groove* and *New Jack City*. Jackson and McHenry, as directors, would once again be at the helm of a successful project, and in the process, make the first movie sequel of the Black Film Renaissance of 1991.

IVY LEAGUE BACKGROUNDS

Unlike many of the New Jack filmmakers, McHenry and Jackson took a more traditional path to the director's chair. They entered the entertainment industry from the business side of production and moved toward the creative end. Both men attended Ivy League schools which, among other things, certainly prepared them to rise through the corporate ranks of the Hollywood studios.

Doug McHenry, who grew up in Oakland, California, studied economics at Stanford University where he was an honors student. McHenry also attended Harvard's Business and Law Schools. McHenry's counterpart, George Jackson, grew up in Harlem and attended Harvard University as an undergraduate.

THEY PAID THEIR DUES BEHIND THE SCENES

Both McHenry and Jackson built their early careers behind the scenes in a variety of jobs. McHenry got his start as an assistant to movie producer Peter Guber. He soon moved on to greater leadership positions with the company Casablanca Filmworks. At Casablanca, McHenry was the Head of Business Affairs and had a hand in the creation of several movies including *Foxes, Hollywood Knights, Midnight Express,* and a film of the disco music era called *Thank God Its Friday.*

Rising quickly up the executive ladder, McHenry became Vice President of Production at a modest sized production company, AVCO Embassy Pictures. As a V.P. with AVCO, McHenry worked on the development and production of two horror films, *Prom Night* and *Scanners,* and a comedy, *This Is Spinal Tap* which launched the directorial career of former TV actor Rob Reiner ("Meathead" from *All In The Family).* Reiner would later direct a number of successful films including *Misery* and *A Few Good Men).*

McHenry soon rose to become president of several companies including Solar Films where he produced a number of music videos for African American artists including *The Whispers* and *Midnight Star.* In addition to a stint producing music videos, McHenry became the president of AVCO Embassy's Television division and was involved in the production of television shows for both the networks and cable television.

JACKSON GOT HIS START IN TELEVISION

Like McHenry, George Jackson had a busy early career. As a producer trainee at Paramount Studios, he had the opportunity to work on shows like *Laverne & Shirley* and *The New Odd Couple,* which featured black leading men. After learning the ropes with several of Paramount's television programs, Jackson became an assistant to Universal Pictures film executive Thom Mount.

During the early 1980s actor/comedian Richard Pryor formed a production company called Indigo under the auspices of Columbia Pictures which hired Jackson as the President of Production. During the short existence of Indigo, Jackson was instrumental in cultivating projects with a number of young black filmmakers such as Reginald Hudlin, Spike Lee, and Robert Townsend. None of the Indigo productions came to fruition, but each of these filmmakers benefitted in some way from the initial interest and help from the company.

THE JACKSON/MCHENRY PARTNERSHIP IS FORMED

In 1985 George Jackson teamed up with Doug McHenry and the duo began to produce a number of TV and film projects. Their 1985 movie *Krush Groove,* directed by Michael Schultz, became a big hit. McHenry and Jackson would then produce several TV programs for the networks including the summer replacement series for ABC, *New Attitude.* As a producing team they would make another film together, directed by Michael Schultz, called *Disorderlies* (1987).

NEW JACK BECOMES THEIR BIGGEST HIT

After years of producing projects for other companies, the two men began the 1990s with the formation of their own business, Jackson/McHenry Productions. For their first production they chose a script about a New York drug dealer. After hiring journalist/screenwriter Barry Michael Cooper, who is credited with creating the word "New Jack," the screenplay evolved into a contemporary gangster drama called *New Jack City.* Jackson and McHenry also selected Mario Van Peebles as the director of the film.

New Jack City became an enormous hit for Jackson/McHenry Productions. The 1991 film, distributed by Warner Brothers, was produced with a budget of $8.5 million and grossed over $47 million. The monetary and critical success of the film solidified the producing duo's position in Hollywood. For their follow-up to *New Jack City* Jackson and McHenry choose to take the reigns of another successful film, as directors of the sequel to a 1990 hit, *House Party.*

TAG TEAM DIRECTORS

Not only was *House Party 2* the first sequel of the New Jack era, it also was also the only film of this period to be directed by two people. The convention with the majority of Hollywood films is that there is only one director in charge of a production. Jackson and McHenry, however, worked as a successful team in the past and when the time came to direct, they brought their partnership to that position as well. As team directors, the duo took turns overseeing different aspects of the film. At times Jackson would direct the dance sequences, and his partner George often took over when it came time for dramatic scenes.

THE *PARTY* MOVES TO COLLEGE

The script for *House Party 2,* written by African American actor/writer Rusty Cundieff, retained the main cast of the original film and placed them in a college setting. In the sequel, the story continues with "Kid" (Christopher Reid) and his girlfriend "Sidney" (Tisha Campbell) as they depart their neighborhood for college. Kid's father "Pop" (Robin Harris) has passed away (as did the actor Harris after the release of the first film), but his presence is still felt. In the absence of his father, Kid's church gives him a send off for school including a tuition check. Kid's best friend Play, now the manager of a record store, finds the tuition check that Kid has misplaced and he is subsequently swindled out of the funds by an unscrupulous record producer played by actress/model Iman. In an effort to earn back the lost money, Play organizes a pajama party, or a "pajama jammy jam," as he calls it, at Kid's college in the faculty dining hall. The D.J. for the evening is "Bilel," played by Martin Lawrence, another member of the original cast. Like the first film, Kid and Play perform a rap number and are featured in a big dance number.

"EDUTAINMENT"—PUTTING A MESSAGE IN THEIR MOVIE

Like the first *House Party,* which targeted a teen audience, Jackson and McHenry wanted to include important messages within the context of an entertaining movie. They often used the word "Edutainment" to describe their blend of education and entertainment.

Jackson and McHenry tackled the issue of affirmative action and minority students through a professor in the film played by actor George Stanford Brown. The professor cautions Kid, who is inattentive in class, to study harder because as a black student, others may assume he was admitted to college only due to the color of his skin and not because of his intellect.

Among the other educational messages is one of self-identity. Sydney's roommate, played by rapper/actress Queen Latifah, encourages her to take courses dealing with black history. She also suggests that Sydney spend more time thinking about her studies and less about her boyfriend, Kid.

ANOTHER HIT FOR JACKSON/MCHENRY

House Party 2, which was shot on a budget of $4.5 million, almost double that of the first film, grossed over $19.2 million during its 1991 release. Although it did not gross as much as the original movie, over $27 million, its box office earnings were about 70% of the first film, which many in Hollywood would consider to be quite good for a sequel.

MORE PROJECTS WAITING IN THE WINGS

After successfully directing *House Party 2,* Jackson and McHenry returned to their roles as producers and focused their attention on a number of other projects they had in development. Foremost was a planned sequel to their 1991 hit, New Jack City. In addition, the duo was also developing a project for the cable network HBO about the Black Panther political party of the late 1960s.

By 1993 Jackson and McHenry landed a lucrative deal with a newly formed distribution company, Savoy Films. Their agreement with Savoy permitted the duo to produce six movies of their choosing with an average budget of $12 million each.

In addition to the Savoy contract, Jackson and McHenry began preparations to produce *House Party 3* for New Line Cinema. Rappers Kid 'N Play were scheduled to reprise their roles for a third time, with a bachelor party featured in the story.

21 Strictly Business

Kevin Hooks: Director

(Warner Bros., 1991)

HE GREW UP IN THE INDUSTRY

Although actor/director Kevin Hooks joined the ranks of Hollywood's New Jack directors in 1991 with *Strictly Business*, his feature film directorial debut, he practically grew up in the entertainment industry. As a child actor Hooks was featured in a variety of roles. Of note, at the age of nine, he appeared with his father, veteran actor Robert Hooks, in a TV series called *N.Y.P.D.*. Young Kevin also starred in the acclaimed CBS children's program, J.T.. The role which Hooks is probably best remembered for is the 1972 film *Sounder* in which he portrayed the son of Southern sharecroppers, played by Paul Winfield and Cicely Tyson.

As Hooks grew up, so did his on-screen roles. During the late 1970s he was featured as part of an ensemble cast in the CBS series *The White Shadow*, about a white basketball coach and his all-black, high school team. His experience and contacts made behind the scenes on that show would later lead to a chance to broaden his career.

DIRECTING ELSEWHERE MARKS A NEW CAREER

While acting in The White Shadow, Hooks made friends with Grant Tinker, a production company executive responsible for the show. That friendship translated into Hooks' first directing job in 1982 with the NBC series *St. Elsewhere*. The weekly hospital drama, which featured Denzel Washington as part of the cast, was a product of Grant Tinker's company, MTM. Tinker was also the President of NBC and his son Mark served as one of the writer/producers of the show.

Not willing to give up either career, Hooks continued to both act and direct whenever possible. He would next direct *Roots: The Gift*, a special holiday TV movie broadcast on ABC which featured characters from the network's highly successful *Roots* mini-series of 1977.

Returning to work in front of the camera, Hooks would appear in a short-lived, 1986 TV comedy series called *He's the Mayor,* about a young man dealing with the problems of running a city with a staff of misfits. In the same year he would direct the TV program *Teen Father* as part of the ABC *Afternoon Special* series for young people. The show chronicled the challenges faced by a teenage boy who fathers a child, then learns to care for the infant. Hooks was later nominated for an Emmy award for his direction of *Teen Father.* The Emmy nomination was one of three that Hooks would eventually receive for his work as a director.

DIRECTING EPISODIC TV SHOWS

After beginning his directing career with *St. Elsewhere,* Hooks soon amassed a number of other TV directing credits. He directed several episodes of the critically acclaimed ABC law show *Equal Justice,* produced by another African American actor turned director, Thomas Carter *(Swing Kids,* 1993). In addition, Hooks directed episodes of NBC's dramatic series, *Midnight Caller.*

HOOKS WINS ACE FOR *HEATWAVE*

Not only was he in demand to direct network television shows, Hooks was also selected to helm a variety of made for cable programs such as HBO's *Vietnam War Stories.* In 1990 he won cable television's highest honor the Ace Award for his direction of the dramatic movie *Heatwave.* The two-hour film was produced by the TNT cable network and starred Blair Underwood. In the movie, based upon real events, Underwood portrayed a black man working for the Los Angeles Times who became an on-the-scene reporter during the Watts, California riots of the late 60s.

THE CHANCE TO DIRECT A FEATURE FILM

Kevin Hooks got his chance to direct *Strictly Business* after the original director Rolando Hudson was fired. Hudson was initially hired because he was a friend of the film's producer, African American recording industry executive, Andre Harrell. The production company backing the project did not want Harrell to hire a first-time director like Hudson. The company agreed to give Hudson just four days to prove himself. Unfortunately, he was unable to please the company executives and as a result was promptly fired after four days. Hooks was then hired based upon his successful track record as a television director.

FROM *BEVERLY* TO *BUSINESS*

During the course of production, the film Hooks was directing had the working title *Go Beverly*. The story, developed by producer Andre Harrell and written by Pam Gibson and Nelson George, had at its center a young, care-free woman named "Beverly" played by Halle Berry. Beverly's name was later changed to "Natalie" and the film underwent a title change as well. Eventually, the movie was renamed *Strictly Business* to highlight the business deal at the heart of the film.

The deal is initiated by an upwardly mobile black corporate executive, "Waymond Tisdale III," portrayed by Joseph Phillips. Tisdale notices the lovely Natalie in a restaurant one day and instantly falls in love. Tisdale, upon finding that a company mailroom worker named "Bobby Johnson" (Tommy Davidson) knows Natalie, seeks Johnson's help to meet her. Bobby insists that Tisdale become more street-wise in his style of dress and way of speaking in order to win Natalie's heart. In exchange, Tisdale provides Bobby with a position in the corporate trainee program. After giving Tisdale a personality make-over, Bobby takes him to nightclubs in search of Natalie.

AFTER *BUSINESS* HOOKS LANDS *PASSENGER*

Strictly Business opened on November 8, 1991 and was the last film to be released during the Black Film Renaissance of that year. Unfortunately, it was met with mixed reviews and lackluster attendance at movie theaters. It grossed only $7.7 million theatrically, which was disappointing given the film's estimated cost, somewhere between $4.5 and $6 million.

As for director Kevin Hooks, he had a number of projects lined up, the first of which was to be an action-adventure film starring Wesley Snipes called *Passenger 57*.

PART THREE:

The New Jack Spirit Continues

22 Daughters of the Dust

Julie Dash: Producer/Writer/Director

(Kino International, 1992)

SHE EARNED A PLACE IN HISTORY

Filmmaker Julie Dash became a significant part of cinema history during the beginning of 1993 with the release of her feature film *Daughters of the Dust. Daughters,* which was her feature film directorial debut, established Dash as the first African American woman to have a film distributed to theaters on a national basis in the United States.

Prior to Dash, the only other black female director to have a film in major release was Eulzan Palcy, a native of the French speaking East West Indies island, Martinique. Palcy directed the 1989 anti-apartheid drama *A Dry White Season.* Given that the focus of this book is on contemporary African American film directors of the United States, Palcy was not included.

A FILM 16 YEARS IN THE MAKING

Although Dash made history with the release of *Daughters,* getting the film made was no easy task. It took her 16 years to bring the completed project to fruition. She began development of the script in 1976 while a student at the American Film Institute (AFI). It was during this time that she began to develop a story based, in part, upon her own family history. Her father's ancestors were people who came to the United States from West Africa. They were enslaved and brought to port towns along the islands off the coast of Georgia and South Carolina. After emancipation her ancestors settled in that coastal region, commonly known as the Sea Islands.

It was Dash's desire to create a story about African American women at the turn of the century. Her film would feature descendants of West Africans who developed their own language known as "Gullah." Initially, Dash thought of the film as a short film, but as she began to conduct further research, the need for a longer project became apparent.

THE TEENAGE FILMMAKER

Dash, who grew up in the Queensbridge housing projects in Long Island City, New York, began her path as a filmmaker in 1968. At the age of 17, while attending a workshop with a friend at the Studio Museum in Harlem, she had the opportunity to learn about filmmaking.

Although Dash developed an interest in filmmaking while in high school, she entered college as a physical education major at the City College of New York (CCNY). Eventually, she changed her degree program to filmmaking and became a student in the David Picker Film Institute at CCNY. After graduating with a B.A. in film production she decided to continue her studies at one of the nation's top film schools, the University of California at Los Angeles (UCLA). Dash was not accepted into UCLA as one of her professors failed to submit a letter of recommendation to the school.

Not wanting to give up on her dream of becoming a filmmaker, Dash continued her education with practical experience by joining the crew of an independent film called *Passing Through* which was shot in the California desert.

DAUGHTERS IS BORN IN COLLEGE

Dash would soon return to school as she applied for and received a fellowship to attend the American Film Institute in California. While at the AFI, Dash began to develop an idea for a short film about African American women that later became *Daughters*. Her project received a real boost in 1981 when she landed a Guggenheim grant to develop films about African American women. By 1983 Dash had completed a period film called *Illusions*. It was set in World War II and starred African American actress Lonette McKee as a movie studio executive who passes for a white woman.

During her time at AFI Dash began to look to her own family as the basis for another film about women. She soon found, however, that several people in her family did not want to discuss some of their more personal stories. This proved to be a short lived inconvenience for Dash as she began to research African Americans, like her family, who populated the Eastern coastal islands at the turn of the century. Dash gathered a large amount of information, so much so that she believed it merited a feature length film. Drawing from both her research and her family history, Dash began to fashion a fictional story into a script by 1985.

AMERICAN PLAYHOUSE PROVIDED INITIAL FUNDING

With just enough grant money to begin a bare bones production, Dash traveled to one of the coastal islands in 1987 and shot a short, 10 minute "demo reel," consisting of sample scenes from her script, which gave potential investors an idea of what she was trying to create.

Despite the fact that many Hollywood executives were impressed with Dash's short film, they were unwilling to take a chance on funding her project, as it was not like the conventional stories about black people that Hollywood usually produced. After an intensive search for money, Dash reached many dead-ends. By 1988 the situation improved for the better, when Dash met Lynn Holst, the director of program development for the PBS series *American Playhouse*. Holst believed in the project and arranged for *Playhouse* to put up a majority of the money to produce Dash's film.

THE SEA ISLAND SHOOT

Just as production was about to begin in October of 1989, Hurricane Hugo ravaged the coastal region where Dash was scheduled to shoot. This caused the production to be delayed by about a week.

The island location itself presented a challenge for Dash and her production team because the area was designated as protected beachfront property by the government. This prevented the crew from bringing heavy, and potentially damaging, lighting equipment onto the island. As a result, Dash's cinematographer, Arthur Jaffe, made use of the natural sunlight. Jaffe and Dash took advantage of the sun at different times of day, thus forcing them to wait or hurry to capture a particular quality of light. Despite the difficulty of a rushed production, shot entirely outdoors, Dash completed the shooting in a total of 28 days with a budget of about $100,000.

She began to edit the film in her home during January of 1990. It took almost a year to complete the editing as she had to continue raising money to support the postproduction of her film.

THE STRUGGLE FOR DISTRIBUTION

Dash had a great deal of difficulty finding a willing distributor as many companies did not believe there was a market for her film. Several distributors even told her that African Americans would not want to see her film.

By January 1991, undeterred by the lack of support from distributors, Dash began to enter *Daughters* in film festivals across the country hoping to attract a distribution deal. That strategy paid off when the film became a hit at the 1991 Sundance Film Festival in Utah and walked off with the "Best Cinematography" award. A U.S. distribution deal followed in September 1991 when a small New York distributor, Kino International, agreed to handle the film. Kino usually distributed foreign films, a fact congruent with the perception by many that *Daughters* appeared to be very much like a foreign film. Perhaps this was due, in part, to it's depiction of a facet of African American culture that had never been seen before on the screen.

A SOLD OUT SUCCESS STORY

Daughters of the Dust opened on January 18, 1992 at the Film Forum theater in New York City. Favorable word of mouth quickly spread and screenings were frequently sold out. The distributor, Kino International, then opened the film across the country one city at a time. The gradual release schedule provided Dash with an opportunity to travel to many cities to promote her film with the help of an African American public relation company, KJM 3.

Daughters would eventually go on to gross over $2 million in theaters. The film was exposed to an even wider audience when it aired in 1993 on PBS as part of the American Playhouse series.

Due to the success of *Daughters,* Hollywood studios began to express an interest in Julie Dash. During 1993 she used that interest to offer ideas of the kinds of films she wanted to direct, but unfortunately, Hollywood executives were not interested.

Note to the reader: For a full account on the making of *Daughters of the Dust,* I recommend that you read *Daughters of the Dust: The Making of an African American Woman's Film* by Julie Dash, published by The New Press, 1992.

23

Juice

Ernest R. Dickerson: Writer/Director

(Paramount, 1992)

A MIDDLE-AGED DIRECTOR WITH JUICE

A 40 year old filmmaker named Ernest Dickerson made the transition from cinematographer to director in 1992 with his debut film, *Juice*, a gritty tale of four young black men growing up surrounded by inner city violence. Prior to Juice Dickerson was known primarily as director Spike Lee's exclusive cinematographer. Dickerson's skillful camera work, compositions, and lighting designs stood out in Lee's six feature films, from *She's Gotta Have It* to the epic *Malcolm X*. Of note, his work on Lee's *Do The Right Thing* garnered the 1989 Film Critics Award for cinematography.

SCHOOL DAYS AT HOWARD UNIVERSITY

Dickerson's path to filmmaking was initially indirect as he enrolled in Howard University's architecture program during 1972. He developed an appreciation for the photographic image while working as a photographer for Howard's student newspaper, *The Hilltop*. In addition to majoring in architecture, Dickerson also took classes in the film department where he learned about cinematography and eventually made the decision to pursue a career in filmmaking.

DICKERSON AND SPIKE LEE AT NYU

After graduating from Howard in 1977 with a degree in architecture, Dickerson stayed in the Washington area for a few years working as a medical photographer. In 1979 he entered the graduate film program at New York University (NYU). It was at NYU where Dickerson met Spike Lee. The duo began to work together during their second year at NYU on Lee's student film, Sarah (1981). Dickerson served as Lee's cinematographer and they continued to work together throughout their NYU days. Lee's thesis film *Joe's Bed-Stuy Barbershop: We Cut Heads* (1982) served as the launching pad for Dickerson's professional career. *Joe's* won a student academy award for Lee and led to a big cinematography job for Dickerson on director John Sayles' feature, *The Brother from Another Planet* (1984).

WORKING AS A PROFESSIONAL CINEMATOGRAPHER

After working on the Sayles film, Dickerson went on to photograph not only Spike Lee's first six feature films, but films for other directors like Michael Schultz *(Krush Groove,* 1985), and Robert Townsend *(Eddie Murphy: Raw,* 1987). Dickerson's body of work also includes several episodic television shows, *Tales from the Darkside* and *Law and Order,* music videos for artists like Anita Baker, Miles Davis, and Bruce Springsteen, and several television commercials directed by his longtime collaborator, Spike Lee.

In addition to being the only African American admitted to the professional union for cinematographers, the American Society of Cinematographers (ASC), Dickerson, in 1990, at age 38 became the youngest member of that prestigious organization.

THE BEGINNING OF HIS DIRECTING CAREER

Juice was not Dickerson's first foray into directing on a professional level. In 1990 he directed an edition of the PBS series *Great Performances* called *Spike & Co.: Do It A Cappella.* The one-hour special, co-hosted by Lee and actress/director Debbie Allen, profiled the performances of several a cappella groups.

THE 8 YEAR DEVELOPMENT OF JUICE

Dickerson's feature film directorial debut, *Juice,* was a project that was years in the making. He co-wrote the original script, with his friend Gerard Brown, eight years prior to its production. Brown also wrote and co-executive produced Dickerson's *Spike & Co. PBS* show. The duo were inspired to draft the story for *Juice,* a slang term meaning power and respect, because they were struck by the extremely violent world in which inner city children were growing up in. Given their violent environment, these children often went to extremes to get "juice," the respect of their peers.

Dickerson was reluctant to move forward with the film for several reasons. First, he began to work professionally as a cinematographer after graduating from NYU. Secondly, the script was in its initial draft stage and he was concerned that children might find the violent character "Bishop" to be more appealing than the other characters. So, he shelved the script until he found time to develop a positive character "Q" to balance Bishop.

When Dickerson decided to move forward with the project in early 1991 four movie studios expressed an interest in buying the script, however, they each wanted to make changes in the story. Namely, they wanted to revamp the script and make it into more of a comedy. Dickerson declined their offers and continued to seek creative control over his project elsewhere.

HOW *JUICE* FINALLY GOT MADE

The script was eventually picked up by a group of white, independent producers, partners Neal H. Moritz and David Heyman and their co-producer Peter Frankfurt. The producers agreed with Dickerson's wishes that the film be produced on location in New York with an unknown cast and on a tight budget. The producers went right to work and acquired funding from Island World Productions, an independent production company from London. Island World set the budget at $3 million and arranged a six-week production schedule. Dickerson then rolled cameras in March of 1991.

PARAMOUNT MAKES MARKETING CHANGES

Before *Juice* was released in theaters, Paramount Pictures, the film's distributor, made a change in the poster which would be used for advertisements. In the original poster the character Bishop was pictured with a jacket hood drawn around his head. He held a serious, almost worried expression on his face, while looking slightly over his shoulder at his three friends, Q, Raheem, and Steel. Bishop also held a small gun in the ad and that is where Paramount made the change. Before the film's release the gun was airbrushed from the character's hand. The alteration was made, according to Harry Anderson (Paramount's vice president of communications), because "a decision was made by our marketing people that the image of the four friends was strong enough without the gun" (Washington Post, Feb. 2, 1992, p. G 8).

Ernest Dickerson, the film's director, went on record with his displeasure over Paramount's decision to change the poster, "Bruce Willis gets the gun and Damon Wayans gets the football (in *The Last Boy Scout* ads)...I don't think seeing an image of a black with a gun is going to make someone run out and shoot somebody else" (USA Today, Jan. 15, 1992, p. 1 D).

DICKERSON PLOTS HIS FUTURE AS A DIRECTOR

With over ten years of highly acclaimed work as a cinematographer, coupled with the maturity of entering his 40s, Ernest Dickerson had a successful debut film behind him and was truly poised to begin his career as a director.

After the completion of *Juice,* Dickerson returned to directing music videos and joined the staff of Original Film, a bi-coastal production company, as a director of television commercials. Dickerson made the move into commercials in an effort to keep active on a professional and creative basis while developing feature film projects. At Original Film, Dickerson made plans to serve as both cinematographer and director on commercials and public service announcements whenever possible.

The November 1992 release of *Malcolm X* marked a high point in the decade long working relationship between Spike Lee and Ernest Dickerson. *Malcolm X,* a project the two once discussed and dreamed about doing while at NYU, became reality as their sixth and perhaps last feature film together. With the completion of his directorial debut, *Juice,* a year prior to *Malcolm,* it became clear that although Dickerson expressed an interest in working with Lee again, his directing schedule might prevent future collaborations.

As a follow-up to *Juice,* Dickerson wanted to try something different and direct a science fiction script about African Americans called *Future Crimes,* but found that the studios were unwilling to back the film. Although his futuristic project was turned down, he was approached with a number of other scripts to direct, but they failed to capture his attention as he found many of them focused on the same themes he explored in *Juice.*

In 1993 Dickerson had selected his next directing project, a film for New Line Cinema called *Surviving the Game.* The story concerned a group of men seeking the thrill of a hunt by chasing a homeless man, played by rapper/actor Ice-T, through the wilderness.

24 One False Move

Carl Franklin: Director

(IRS Releasing, 1992)

THE FILM THAT ALMOST DISAPPEARED

Director Carl Franklin learned his craft in the latter 1980s by directing several low budget features for the modern day king of low budget films, producer Roger Corman. By 1990 Franklin had completed his biggest and perhaps best project, an independent film called *One False Move*. Unfortunately, the movie was heading for obscurity, much like his previous low-budget work. Just when it appeared that the film was destined for failure, movie critics revived interest in the project and began to champion both Franklin and his work. Franklin, who was just beginning his career as a director, found himself in demand at the age of 43.

FROM FOOTBALL TO FLOODLIGHTS

Franklin grew up as the youngest of three children during the 1960s in a tough neighborhood in Richmond, California. In 1967 he had the opportunity to leave his violent environment when he was accepted into the University of California at Berkeley on a football scholarship. Upon the urging of friends on the football team he enrolled in a dramatic arts class because it served as an easy English course requirement. It was also rumored to be a good way to meet women. What initially seemed like a great opportunity to find romance turned into a career choice as Franklin excelled in the drama class. While at Berkeley several alumni suggested that he go to New York to pursue a career in acting.

Franklin heeded the advice of his mentors and made his way to New York. He soon began to find work in theatrical productions in both New York and Washington, D.C. Of note, Franklin acted in the prestigious New York Shakespeare Festival at the Joseph Papp Public Theater in 1971.

While pursuing roles on stage he also worked in film and television. Franklin was featured in the 1973 film, *Five on the Black Hand Side.* Soon after, he landed a part on a detective show called "Caribe" which barely lasted through the 1974 television season.

THE *A-TEAM* CHANGED HIS CAREER

By the early 1980s Franklin was playing "Captain Crane," a character featured on NBC's action series *The A-Team.* After two seasons Franklin left the show as he found the program to be far too "cartoonish" in nature, given his training as a theater actor. Upset with the quality of roles he was offered on television shows, Franklin quit acting for four years. During that time he decided to refocus his energy behind the camera as a director.

PUNK GARNERS ATTENTION

To fulfill his new goal in life, Franklin enrolled in the directing program at the American Film Institute (AFI) in 1986. While at the AFI he directed a short thesis film called *Punk,* a story about a nine year old boy from South Central Los Angeles, who kills a child abuser. Low-budget movie producer Roger Corman saw the film and recognized Franklin's potential as a director. Corman then hired the filmmaker to direct three films for his production company, Concorde Films. The movies were not of the best quality, but they helped Franklin pay for his education.

HIRED TO HELM *HURRICANE*

Another producer Jesse Beaton was impressed with Franklin's thesis film. She subsequently interviewed him for a job to direct a screenplay by Tom Epperson and Billy Bob Thornton called *Hurricane.* The script dealt with a trio of Los Angeles drug dealers who commit a brutal murder of another dealer and the innocent members of his family. The three killers then evade the police by fleeing across the country, with a detour to Arkansas because a woman in the group wishes to see her child one last time. The story concludes in Arkansas as the gang meets its match when they encounter a Sheriff nicknamed "Hurricane."

Franklin was hired to direct the project as the producer, Beaton, believed he had what younger directors lacked, the maturity to understand the complex characters in what otherwise might have been a conventional action film.

The screenplay, as written by Epperson and Thornton, was on the surface a crime thriller, yet, at its core was a story of relationships. The relationships centered around an African American woman named "Fantasia," her white boyfriend, and leader of the violent group, "Ray," and later, characters that we meet in Fantasia's fictional hometown, Star City, Arkansas.

FRANKLIN MAKES *FALSE MOVE*

Franklin brought additional nuances to the script by selecting both white and black actors for the major characters. The lead female role of Fantasia went to an African American, Cynda Williams, whose screen debut was *Mo' Better Blues*. Her white co-star, Billy Bob Thornton, who also co-wrote the screenplay, played Fantasia's boyfriend "Ray." The casting of Thornton and Cynda Williams proved to generate chemistry between the co-stars as they were married upon completion of the film. The role of the third member of the gang, the cold-blooded intellectual of the group named "Pluto," went to another African American actor, Michael Beach. Bill Paxton, known for his work as a marine in the film *Aliens,* rounded out the cast as Sheriff "Hurricane" Dixon.

In 1990 Franklin started production on *Hurricane,* which later came to be known as *One False Move,* with a budget of $2.5 million. The funding came from two sources, a production company called IRS Media and Columbia/Tri-Star's home video division.

Once shooting of the film was completed in December of 1990, all involved with the project believed it would, like many low-budget films, be released straight to home video and not in theaters. However, the producers were impressed with the final product as crafted by Franklin and they were committed enough to see the film succeed. Since the project had no major stars to attract moviegoers, a plan was formed to help draw attention to the film.

The distributor IRS Media chose to release *One False Move* initially in only three cities, Chicago, Los Angeles, and Seattle, during May and June of 1992. Chicago and Los Angeles were chosen due to the influential film critics located in those cities. Seattle was selected as Franklin and his producer, Jesse Beaton, were in the area shooting a movie for the cable network HBO. The local press was invited to the location to interview both Franklin and Beaton.

The strategy behind the limited release worked quite well as the film grossed over $400,000 in one month in just a few cities. Sheila Benson, then a critic for *The Los Angeles Times,* wrote a favorable review about the film and went on to present it at the Floating Film Festival. At the festival, *Chicago Sun Times* critic Roger Ebert saw the film and was so impressed that he touted it both in print and on his nationally syndicated TV show, *Siskel & Ebert.*

Since there was no television advertising for *One False Move,* the strong box office attendance of the film could be attributed primarily to both favorable reviews and audience word-of-mouth. By its second month of release, it opened in an additional 15 cities. Due to its success in other cities, the film was released for a second time in both Los Angeles and New York.

Franklin was quickly recognized in the film industry for his talent as he received a flood of offers to direct other scripts. But before he could consider what his next project would be, Franklin was busy completing a mini-series for HBO. The three hour series, titled *Laurel Avenue,* was about a turbulent weekend in the lives of an African American family. The series aired on HBO during July of 1993, and was often shown as a double-bill with *One False Move.*

Even Franklin's student thesis film *Punk* reached a larger audience during this time, as it was aired nationally on PBS stations in 1993 as part of the *Alive TV* series. With his work on *Laurel Avenue* finished, Franklin began to sift through the many scripts sent to him from the major Hollywood studios. He was offered a variety of directing assignments from thrillers to science fiction. With so many scripts to choose from, the ball was definitely in Carl Franklin's court as he prepared for his follow-up to *One False Move.*

25 Deep Cover

Bill Duke: Director

(New Line Cinema, 1992)

DUKE RETURNS TO THE POLICE BEAT

Bill Duke's second project as a feature film director, called *Deep Cover,* provided him with the opportunity to once again deal with the subject of urban law enforcement. Duke began his directing career with episodic television programs, among them, police dramas like *Hill St. Blues* and *Cagney and Lacey*.

Deep Cover starred Laurence Fishburne as "Russell Stevens, Jr.," a young Los Angeles police officer who is recruited by the Drug Enforcement Agency (DEA) to go undercover to catch a major drug dealer. While undercover, Fishburne's character is pulled into a lucrative life of crime by a lawyer/drug dealer played by actor Jeff Goldblum.

ORIGINALLY WRITTEN FOR A WHITE ACTOR

Duke was selected to direct the project as the producers believed he was well suited for a film that was targeted specifically at an African American audience. Although the final story for *Deep Cover,* as crafted by screenwriter by Michael Tolkin, was written with a black man as the lead character, the script did not begin that way.

The screenplay was originally developed as an undercover police drama by screenwriter Henry Bean and Producer Pierre David; the team that made the successful 1990 police thriller, *Internal Affairs*.

When Bean and David were shopping their script around to the Hollywood studios, an executive at Paramount Pictures suggested that they change the lead role to one that could be played by a black actor. The Paramount exec explained that by changing the lead character to a black man, the studio could then market the film to black moviegoers. Paramount was quite impressed with the success of Spike Lee's 1989 film, *Do The Right Thing,* and was looking to cash in on the lucrative black audience.

Acting on the advice of the Paramount contact, the screenplay for *Deep Cover* was rewritten with a black man at the center of the story. When producers Bean and David presented the revised script to Paramount, they were turned down because the new management at the studio was unwilling to proceed with the project. Bean and David then found that all of the remaining major Hollywood studios also declined to make the film.

TARGETING A BLACK AUDIENCE

By 1991 a small company called New Line Cinema expressed an interest in the *Deep Cover* project. Given the phenomenal success of director John Singleton's first film *Boyz N the Hood,* New Line wanted to use *Deep Cover* as a means to attract African American moviegoers. Their technique of targeting a specific audience was known as "niche marketing." Niche marketing was not a new concept to New Line because they successfully tapped into other specific audiences, like children, with the *Teenage Mutant Ninja Turtle* movies and teenagers with the *Nightmare on Elm Street* horror film series.

DENZEL WASHINGTON TURNS DOWN THE LEAD

Once the deal had been made with New Line, the producers then attempted to land a major black actor for the lead role. Denzel Washington was the first choice, but he declined their offer. The producers and director Bill Duke then decided that an up-and-coming actor, Larry Fishburne, who was featured in *Boyz N the Hood,* would be a believable choice as the undercover cop.

SLOW AT THE THEATERS, BUT HOT ON VIDEO

When *Deep Cover* was released during April 1992 it did not fare well at movie theaters. New Line had hoped to tap into the large black audience that turned out for *Boyz N the Hood,* but it was not able to achieve the same measure of success, perhaps due to the fact that *Deep Cover* may have appealed to an older black audience.

The situation was quite different when the film was released on home video during November of 1992, approximately six months after its theatrical run. After one month in video stores *Deep Cover* had sold over 180,000 copies at a price of $94.98 each. This meant that the studio would potentially gross $17 million in home video sales. It took *Deep Cover* over four months to gross the same amount in theaters. The niche marketing employed by New Line had clearly paid off once the film was discovered by viewers of home videos.

DUKE MOVES ON TO *CEMETERY*

With his second feature film behind him, Bill Duke was ready to begin his next project. For his third feature as a director, Duke was hired by the Disney studio's Buena Vista distribution company to direct a comedy with white characters called *The Cemetery Club.* The film was based upon the play by Ivan Menchell which featured a group of widows who met at a cemetery.

Duke started production during July of 1992 in Pittsburgh, Pennsylvania with a cast that included veteran actresses Diane Ladd, Ellen Burstyn, and Duke's former acting teacher, Academy Award winning actress Olympia Dukakis.

26 Boomerang

Reginald and Warrington Hudlin: Director and Producer, respectively

Be Be's Kids

Reginald and Warrington Hudlin: Executive Producers

(Paramount, 1992)

TWO BIG FILMS RELEASED IN ONE MONTH

July 1992 could be seen as yet another turning point in the careers of Reginald and Warrington Hudlin, better known as "The Hudlin Brothers." On July 1, 1992 their second and biggest feature film to date *Boomerang*, starring comedian Eddie Murphy, opened on 2,400 screens across the nation. In the film, Murphy was featured as a womanizing executive who is reformed after receiving his comeuppance from a woman whom he cannot obtain.Reginald served as director and his brother Warrington was by his side as producer. In its first week *Boomerang* grossed over $23.7 million, one of the biggest openings for a film by a black filmmaker.

By the end of the month *Boomerang* rang up over $50 million at the box office, and the Hudlin brothers were set to release their third film, BeBe's Kids, the first animated feature starring black characters.

ONE OF THE MOST EXPENSIVE BLACK MOVIES

Variety magazine reported that the "official cost" for *Boomerang*, as reported by the studio, Paramount Pictures, was $40 million (July 13, 1992, p. 20). *Variety* went on to estimate that the film probably had a final price tag of $51 million. If one takes either figure into account, *Boomerang* was the most expensive movie helmed by a black filmmaker at that time. The generous budget was due to a number of factors, including expensive location shooting in New York City, coupled with the fact that the film was six days over schedule at an estimated additional cost of $2 to $3 million. One fourth of the budget reportedly went toward the salary of the film's star Eddie Murphy. Murphy's base salary was reportedly $12 million. The huge salary and the size of *Boomerang's* budget was customary by Hollywood's standards for a star of Murphy's magnitude. He could command such a top salary as his movies consistently made money. In the 1980s

Murphy's nine films grossed over $1 billion worldwide for Paramount Pictures. By 1993 Murphy was touted as a leader when it came to the all important opening weekend grosses of his movies. According to *Weekly Variety* (March 15, 1993, p. 1), Eddie Murphy's movies had an average weekend gross of $16,858,715 million.

AN ALL-STAR CAST

Murphy was a fan of Hudlin's work dating back to his early short films like *The Kold Waves.* After the success of *House Party,* Murphy kept the Hudlin brothers in mind for a project that would suit their comedic skills. Such a project was a script called *Boomerang.*

In addition to having Murphy in the lead role, the film also called upon the talents of an all-star black cast. Former television actress Robin Givens portrayed a woman who toys with the affections of Murphy's character. Newcomer Halle Berry played Murphy's love interest while comedians Martin Lawrence and David Alan Grier were cast as Murphy's office buddies. Rounding out the ensemble were two of Hollywood's more eccentric actresses, veteran performer Eartha Kitt, who portrayed a boss that takes advantage of Murphy, and Grace Jones, cast as a high fashion model on the prowl for Murphy's affections.

REHEARSALS HELD AT MURPHY'S HOME

Boomerang went into production in November of 1990, after about two weeks of rehearsals as requested by the Hudlins; a first for Murphy. Using the script only as a blueprint of sorts, the Hudlins encouraged the actors to improvise during rehearsals. Much like the scripting of *House Party,* the improvisation was often incorporated into the final script. As a result of the extensive rehearsals with the cast, many of which were held at Murphy's New Jersey home, the actor found the subsequent filming and camaraderie on the set to be the best he ever experienced on a film.

BEBE'S KIDS BECOMES A REALITY

While *Boomerang* was in production the Hudlins were hard at work on another film that originally was slated to star stand-up comedian Robin Harris of their first film *House Party.* The Hudlins were developing a story based upon a routine Harris became famous for, called *BeBe's Kids.* Harris recounted in his stage routine how he went to pick a woman up for a date, only to discover that she had several of her neighbor's kids with her. The neighbor was a woman called "BeBe." The date becomes a disaster when Harris takes the group to Disneyland and *BeBe's* undisciplined children cause havoc at the amusement park.

The untimely death of Harris in 1990 forced the Hudlins to rethink the project. As a tribute to him they decided to proceed with the effort as an animated feature film. Reggie served as the writer, and both brothers were executive producers. An African American, Bruce Smith, was chosen as the director of the animated project.

A Los Angeles comedian, Faizon Love, was chosen to provide the voice of Robin Harris. His co-star, actress Vanessa Bell Calloway was cast as the voice of "Jamika," Robin's love interest in the animated film. Calloway spoke to Robin Harris when BeBe's Kids was initially being developed and suggested that she should be his co-star. After Harris' death, Calloway auditioned for the role of "Jamika." She was eventually chosen to be the voice of Jamika, despite the fact that she did not tell the director and producers that Harris originally wanted her for the part.

A SERIES OF CINEMATIC FIRSTS

With *House Party* the Hudlins became the first African-American filmmakers to release a film in the 1990s. Their follow-up films also served as cinematic first. *Boomerang* was the most expensive black film to date with the largest gross earnings as well, $66.6 million by Labor Day 1992, the customary end of the summer movie season. Their third film, *BeBe's Kids,* made bit of cinematic history as the first animated feature starring black characters.

With two films opening in one month, it was quite clear that the Hudlin brothers were a hot property. In the two short years since their debut film, *House Party,* burst onto the Hollywood scene, the Hudlins had clearly established themselves as filmmakers with a winning track record.

Passenger 57

Kevin Hooks: Director

27

(Warner Bros., 1992)

HOOKS LANDS PASSENGER AS A FOLLOW-UP

Actor turned director Kevin Hooks followed up his 1991 directorial debut, *Strictly Business*, with the action/thriller *Passenger 57*. The film starred Wesley Snipes as "John Cutter," an airline anti-terrorist expert who happens to be on board the same plane as international terrorists. P57 was significant for both Snipes and director Hooks as it was the first truly big budget action film to be headed up by black men. A year earlier, Denzel Washington broke into the action film arena with his film *Ricochet*, but he did so without a black director. Wesley Snipes, upon being offered the lead role in P57, reportedly asked for and was given a black director, Kevin Hooks.

SNIPES BECOMES A HOT TICKET

With P57 Snipes had secured his spot among the ranks of leading men. In the 1980s he quickly moved from small parts in movies like *Wildcats*, a high school football comedy, and the hit baseball farce *Major League*, to back-to-back films with director Spike Lee. In Lee's *Mo' Better Blues*, Snipes had a supporting role to the film's star, Denzel Washington, but on the next Lee film, the interracial drama Jungle Fever, he achieved leading man status. His next film, the 1991 smash hit *New Jack City* gave Snipes the chance to pull out all the stops in his portrayal of an inner-city crime boss, and he subsequently drew his share of attention from the Hollywood studios.

PRODUCER PICKS SNIPES AS THE GOOD GUY

Coming off the success of both *Jungle Fever* and *New Jack City*, Snipes was approached with the script for *Passenger 57*. Upon reading the story about a hijacker, who's plot is foiled by a airline security man, Snipes assumed the producers wanted him to portray the villain. To his surprise, producer Lee Rich asked him to play the hero as he believed Snipes was just right for the role. The script was then rewritten to make the lead character a black man. Martial arts were also incorporated into the hero's fight scenes as Snipes had extensive training in that art form.

A FAST TAKE OFF AT THE BOX OFFICE

Passenger 57 was made on a modest budget for an action film, $15 million. The producer of the movie, Lee Rich, had a track record of making action films for under $20 million in an effort to maximize profits. *P57* showed early signs of profitability during its opening weekend as it ranked number one at the box office with a gross of $10,513,925, twice the box office receipts of the second place feature that week, which was the action film *Under Siege*. Near the end of its theatrical release, *P57* grossed over $44 million dollars in the U.S. and it later performed very well upon its home video release in 1993.

P57 PROPELS SNIPES

After *Passenger 57,* leading man Wesley Snipes was certainly in demand as he completed several films back-to-back including *Rising Sun,* with co-star Sean Connery, a crime film called *Sugar Hill,* and then on to yet another big budget action film, the futuristic *Demolition Man,* with co-star Sylvester Stallone. Wesley Snipes, in the span of less than one year, went from joining the ranks of action film heroes to co-starring with several veterans of the genre.

HOOKS RETURNS TO TELEVISION

Given the success of *P57,* Kevin Hooks was assured of directing jobs in the future. Instead of directing another feature film, Hooks opted to return to television, where he worked early in his career as an actor. This time Hooks worked behind the camera as the director of a two-hour pilot for CBS's 1993 season called *Irresistible Force.*

28 Malcolm X

Spike Lee: Writer/Director/Actor

(Warner Bros., 1992)

HIS DREAM PROJECT

Spike Lee was perhaps destined to make a film about a man he greatly admired, slain religious leader Malcolm X. As a show of his determination as a filmmaker, Lee even used a quote from Malcolm X, "By any means necessary," at the close of his films.

Although Lee fulfilled a lifelong dream in directing *Malcolm X*, the project did not originate with him. In 1967, two years after the assassination of Malcolm X, a white producer named Marvin Worth acquired the rights to make a film based upon Malcolm's life from his widow, Betty Shebazz. Worth then hired African American poet/writer James Baldwin to write a screen adaptation of the book *The Autobiography of Malcolm X* by Alex Haley. Baldwin disliked his experience of working in the Hollywood system and wrote about it in an essay entitled *The Devil Finds Work*. Although Baldwin finished a screenplay, it was never produced, but was later published under the title *One Day When I Was Lost*.

COUP STAGED FOR 'X' JOB

After Baldwin, a number of other high caliber writers were hired to pen a script, but the project languished for years perhaps due to the fact that Hollywood was not ready to put the life of Malcolm X onto the screen. By the late 1980s the climate had changed, given the success of movies featuring African Americans. In 1989 the project was put on the fast track at Warner Bros. when veteran filmmaker Norman Jewison was set to direct the film. Jewison had dealt with African American subject matter before as he directed the military based drama *A Soldier's Story*. Jewison called upon two of the men he worked closely with on that film, Denzel Washington and playwright Charles Fuller, to serve as lead actor and screenwriter, respectively. It was Fuller's award-winning work for the stage, *A Soldier's Play,* that Jewison had previously adapted for the screen.

As word spread that Jewison would make a film about Malcolm X, Spike Lee quickly set out to lobby for the director's job. Lee took his campaign to the media by suggesting in interviews that he, as a African American director, would be better suited to bring the life of Malcolm to the screen. He went on to meet with Jewison, discussed his passion for the project, and subsequently convinced Jewison to drop out. Lee's battle to capture the director's chair would be only one of many as his dream project came to fruition.

Upon taking over the project Lee dusted off the screenplay written by the late James Baldwin and used portions of it. Lee wanted to give Baldwin screen credit for his script, but Baldwin's estate, which was run by his sister Gloria, declined to permit his name to be used with Lee's film as she believed Lee had rewritten much of the script. Lee instead shared screen credit with another writer that worked on the Baldwin script, Arnold Perl. By early 1991 Lee had finished his version of the screenplay and was ready to begin shooting.

THE INITIAL BUDGET

Warner Bros. negotiated with Lee for a film budgeted at $20 million with a running time of two hours and 20 minutes maximum. To increase the overall budget, the international distribution rights were sold to Largo Entertainment International for $8 million. Lee also contributed $2 million of his three $3 million salary toward the film. The project was then put into production with a total cost of about $30 million. Lee agreed to Warner's terms, with regard to the length and budget, despite the fact that he was determined to make a more expensive, longer film. He simply wanted to get started on the film and get it shot.

LEE'S MARKETING MACHINE

Virtually as soon as he signed the deal with Warner Bros. to direct *Malcolm X,* Lee began to generate publicity about the project. Lee's proven marketing skills dated back to his first film, *She's Gotta Have It,* when he offered buttons and T-shirts touting his movie.

For *Malcolm X,* Lee developed an extremely popular design for hats and shirts with a silver "X" against black. Awareness of the film, and

Malcolm the man, where high among young people, thanks in large part to the "X" merchandise which many wore as a symbol of pride.

Upon release of the film, Lee donated a percentage of the profits from the "X" merchandise to Malcolm's widow, Betty Shabazz.

PROTESTORS RALLY AGAINST LEE

In August 1991, one month before Lee started shooting, he encountered resistance to the project. Poet Amiri Baraka organized a public gathering in Harlem, New York with a small group of people who expressed their concern about how Lee would portray Malcolm X. They had not seen the script, but Baraka and the protesters were against the selection of Lee as the writer/director. Baraka feared that Lee would distort the image of Malcolm's life and try to make it more palatable to a mass audience. Lee viewed the action taken by Baraka to be a personal attack as Lee was a close friend of Baraka's daughter Lisa, who had co-written two books with him.

Also, during the summer before the film opened, Lee was at the center of another controversy when he suggested to the media that African American children should take the day off from school to see his film. Lee cited how he was taken on a class trip to see the musical *The Sound of Music* when he was a child. Lee also thought that his film would be truly worthy of a school outing.

DENZEL PREPS FOR HIS ROLE

After completing work on his first action film *Ricochet,* Denzel Washington began to prepare for his lead role by immersing himself in the speeches and film footage of Malcolm X. He went to New York to visit the areas where Malcolm lived. He studied with members of the Nation of Islam, and he was also instructed about the customs of Islam by orthodox Muslims.

Playing Malcolm X in a feature film was not the first time Washington portrayed the slain leader. In 1981, Washington, then a struggling actor, won the role of Malcolm in the stage play *When the Chickens Come Home to Roost,* a fictional story of a meeting between Malcolm X and Elijah Muhammad, presented by the Negro Ensemble Company. At the time, Washington knew little about Malcolm X. He took the role, he admits, for a chance to act and to earn a paycheck. It was during the run of the play that Washington learned more about Malcolm and came to respect his vision.

THE DIRECTOR DOES HIS HOMEWORK

Like Denzel Washington, Spike Lee did his share of extensive research to prepare for the project. Lee interviewed Malcolm's widow and other family members as well as a number of scholars. Of note, Lee had a private meeting with the current leader of the Nation of Islam, Minister Louis Farrakhan. Farrakhan expressed his concerns to the director about how the founder of the Nation of Islam and Malcolm's mentor, Elijah Muhammad, would be portrayed. This was a sensitive subject to Farrakhan and members of the Nation of Islam as Malcolm X was seen as a traitor by the Nation after Malcolm openly discussed reports that Muhammad had fathered many children from his own secretaries. It is widely believed that because of his split with Muhammad, Malcolm was assassinated by men from the Nation of Islam.

Lee assured Minister Farrakhan that the revered Elijah Muhammad would be depicted in a fair and accurate manner, warts and all. Farrakhan agreed to hold judgement about the film until after it was finished, but he left Lee with a strong warning to be careful about how the life of Muhammad would be depicted on the screen. For his book on the making of *Malcolm X* Lee transcribed a bit of his conversation with Louis Farrakhan, some of which is rather chilling, as Farrakhan's warning to Lee can be viewed as a threat of sorts.

After the film was released Farrakhan denounced Lee's treatment of Elijah Mohammad. In a speech given in February 1993 Farrakhan said, according to United Press International reports, that Lee depicted Elijah Mohammad, "...as a grotesque individual, a man of very low caliber, low morals, a man not really wise, but a man who manipulated people to make people believe he was sent from God." Farrakhan went on to suggest that one should question the motives of both Lee and the Hollywood studio that produced the film, Warner Bros.

COLOR USED TO CONVEY MALCOLM'S LIFE

Malcolm X was not only Lee's biggest film to date in terms of budget and length, but also in its scope. In his attempt to capture the full life span of Malcolm on film, from his early street hustler days to his assassination, Lee and his crew travelled the world.

Cinematographer Ernest Dickerson used light as a means to convey the many moods and periods of Malcolm's life. The young, carefree Malcolm is depicted with warm, orange and yellow, nostalgic colors. The time he spends in prison is shot with cold and harsh, blue tones. In his later years, as he grew to become a national figure, he is lit with a bright, intense light.

STAYING BUSY AFTER *X* SHOOT

In the spring of 1992, upon completing photography on his film, Lee returned to a busy schedule. Not only did he oversee the editing of the huge project, but Lee made time to shoot an ad campaign for the *Nike* athletic shoe company which encouraged racial harmony, and he also accepted a teaching position at Harvard University. Once a week he commuted to the Harvard campus to teach a class about African American cinema. Lee had been invited to become a visiting professor with the school by the chairman of Harvard's Afro-American Studies Department, Henry Louis Gates, Jr.

WARNER BROS. SCREENS *X* DURING RIOTS

Upon completing a rough edited version of the film, Lee flew to Los Angeles to screen it for Warner Bros. executives on April 30, 1992. While they were watching the film, riots broke out in L.A. Four white police officers were acquitted that day in the beating trial of an African American named Rodney King. The event captured international attention as the beating was videotaped by George Holliday, who witnessed the beating from his home.

When the verdict came in, a number of young people set fires and looted stores in a show of anger over the outcome of the trial. Some of the rioting took place near the Warner Bros. studio.

A HOSTILE TAKEOVER

As Lee neared the last stages of editing, he ran into perhaps his greatest obstacle. The firm hired to insure that he would complete the film both on time and on budget, called The Completion Bond Company, cut off his funding during the editing phase. Company officials charged that Lee violated both his budget of $28 million and the agreement as to length of the film, two hours and 20 minutes. The company was set to take over Lee's project, fire his editors, and bring in others to complete the project. It is quite rare for a bond company to take such drastic action with a production. The founder of the Completion Bond Company, Bette Smith, commented to the

New York Times that since 1981, when the company began, it took control of less than five percent of the films bonded. (NYT, Aug. 11, 1991, p. H 11).

The low rate of takeover by bond companies could be attributed to the fact that the studios usually step in to solve any budget problems in an effort to avoid adverse publicity. According to Lee, his studio bosses at Warner Bros. simply declined to pay beyond the original budget. The studio perhaps used the bond company as a way to force Lee to comply with his contract in terms of the budget and the running time of the film.

Unable to pay for the editing himself, Lee quickly devised a plan to complete the film. He discussed that plan in a press conference held on May 19, 1992; which would have been Malcolm's 67th birthday. Before the assembled press Lee talked about his problems concerning the Completion Bond Company and revealed that editing had continued under his control, for about two months after funding was cut off, thanks to the financial contributions of several famous African Americans. Lee called a number of prominent people to ask for donations. The list of contributors included Bill Cosby, Oprah Winfrey, Janet Jackson, Prince, and basketball stars Michael Jordan and Earvin "Magic" Johnson.

A few days after Lee's news conference, Warner Bros. announced that the studio would put forward the money necessary to complete the film. Warner Bros. asserted that they were not pressured by Lee talking to the press. The studio claimed that they had been working on the problem with the bond company for weeks and the timing of their release of additional money was coincidental. It is estimated that Warner Bros. provided upwards of $5 million to complete the project, thus bringing the final budget to approximately $33 million, a figure closer to the amount of money Lee originally wanted.

THE RODNEY KING BEATING VIDEO

A few months prior to the premiere of the film, Lee encountered yet another major problem. He had wanted to open his film with the footage of motorist Rodney King being savagely beaten by members of the L.A. police, intercut with the image of an American flag burning into the shape of an "X". The man who became famous for videotaping the event, George Holliday, agreed to sell Lee the rights to use the video for $50,000. Holliday later hired a new attorney and asked Lee for more money, arguing that the arrangement agreed to by his previous attorney was no longer valid. Holliday sued Lee for $100,000 for copyright infringement. Lee countered sued and the case was settled out of court in November 1992, just one month before the release of the film, for an undisclosed amount.

PERMISSION GRANTED FOR RARE SAM COOKE SONG

One of the brighter spots of the postproduction process occurred when Lee was able to secure permission to use a song by Sam Cooke called "A Change is Gonna Come." Cooke died in 1964 and use of the song was granted by Cooke's estate only to Martin Luther King, Jr. To convince Allen Klein, the man in charge of Cooke's recordings, that he needed the song in the film, Lee screened for Klein the scene he wanted it for, when Malcolm drives to the Audubon Ballroom prior to his assassination there. Klein agreed to allow Lee to use the song in the scene, but the director was restricted from listing the song in the closing credits, or including it in the soundtrack album. Klein donated the $100,000 fee he received from use of the song to the United Negro College Fund.

UNIVERSAL WOOS LEE

As he put the finishing touches on the film, Lee found a secure home for future projects as he was approached by Universal Pictures. Lee went on to sign a multi-year, first-look agreement that would give the studio the first right to anything written, directed, or produced by Lee. He favored the creative freedom that Universal Studios afforded him in the past and he also saw the deal as an opportunity to produce films by young African American filmmakers.

The first project Lee would direct under the Universal contract would be *Crooklyn,* a story about an African American girl growing up in Brooklyn during the 1970s. The story was developed by Lee's sister Joie and brother Cinque.

ALEX HALEY PASSES AWAY

The author of Malcolm's autobiography, Alex Haley, died before Lee's adaption of his book reached theaters, but he did have an opportunity to see the film and expressed his pleasure with it to Lee.

A PREFERENCE FOR BLACK REPORTERS

A few weeks before the film's release, Lee hit a few raw nerves among the white press when he announced that he preferred granting interviews for his film to African American journalists because they were under-represented in newsrooms. Lee pointed out that since it was customary for many Hollywood stars to be selective about the interviews they granted, then he would do likewise and invoke that custom.

TARGETING TWO AUDIENCES

Malcolm X opened on Wednesday, November 18, 1993 in 1,100 theaters, the widest release of a film by Spike Lee at that time. Despite the wide release, Lee and Warner Bros. knew that given the film's length, three hours and 21 minutes, theater owners would only be able to play it perhaps twice a day, thus reducing the money that could be made at the box office. Both parties believed that it would be possible for the film to perform well despite its length, as a year earlier, director Oliver Stone's three hour epic *JFK,* about the assassination of President Kennedy, earned over $69 million during its theatrical run.

In an effort to bring a wide audience to the film, Warner Bros. carefully marketed *Malcolm X* to both African Americans and whites. The studio spent an estimated $10 to $15 million to advertise and market the film. They hired an African American advertising company called Uni-World Group to develop a marketing campaign targeted for African Americans.

After receiving a number of positive reviews, the ad campaign included quotes from prominent national critics in an effort to attract a broader, white audience. The initial film trailer and TV ads for the movie played down the controversial aspects of Malcolm's life in favor of depicting his evolution from a criminal to a Nation of Islam minister and then to that of a peacemaker.

Upon the film's release Warner Bros. gathered research that indicated that *Malcolm X* was attracting a largely older, African

American audience. The studio was determined to have the film reach as wide an audience as possible, especially young moviegoers, one of the largest segments of the moviegoing public.

In January 1993 Warner Bros. offered a rare break to moviegoers as they cut the ticket price in half for people under 21 on Friday of January 18, 1993, in honor of the Martin Luther King, Jr. holiday. The studio had hoped that more young people would attend as a result of the ticket offer.

By the end of 1992, *Malcolm X* had grossed over $41 million, making it one of Lee's highest grossing films to date.

WIN SOME, LOSE SOME

As many had anticipated with a film of its magnitude, *Malcolm X* won its share of awards and honors. Among the more notable, the National Board of Review voted it one of the year's ten best. The prestigious New York Film Critics Circle selected Denzel Washington as best actor. The film was also on the top ten list on 58 out of 106 critics in the United States. Only three other films had more votes in 1992: *Howards End* with 82, *The Player* with 80, and *Unforgiven* with 76.

With regard to Hollywood's top prize for movies, the Academy Award, Lee didn't expect his film to fare very well given his previous experience with the Motion Picture Academy with *Do the Right Thing.* In January of 1993, while promoting his film's release in Italy, Lee accurately predicted that Denzel Washington would be nominated for an Academy Award and that the film would not walk away with any awards. He also predicted that actor/director's Clint Eastwood's western, *Unforgiven,* would win both Best Director and Best Picture Academy Awards, which it did. One Academy nomination that Lee did not predict, which his film received, was for Best Costume Design, but it lost in that category as well.

JAPAN EMBRACES *X*

Interest in Lee's film extended beyond the shores of the United States. Upon its release in Japan, theaters screening the movie were consistently sold out. Lee's chain of stores, "Spike's Joint," had an outlet in Japan which saw brisk business of "X" and other merchandise from Lee's films.

The excitement over Malcolm "Ekkusu" (the Japanese pronunciation of "X") was a direct result of Japan's young people who clamored to learn more about the man through books, videos, and CDs. The film had opened during February 1993, at a time when Japanese teens were extremely interested in African American culture, as rap and hip-hop music had become a big item in their country. The response to the film was so great that a street in Tokyo was renamed "Malcolm X Boulevard."

LEE'S CAREER EVOLVES

After completing the monumental task of bringing the life of Malcolm X to the masses, Lee adopted a slightly slower pace in terms of film production. His passion and commitment to helping other African Americans in the artistic community endured as Lee broadened the scope of business to include television projects, retailing through his chain of *Spike's Joint* stores, and the development of his own record label, *Forty Acres and a Mule Musicworks.*

Using his contract with Universal as a springboard, he helped other African American filmmakers with everything from developing a documentary about Malcolm X to producing the debut films of several new filmmakers.

As the filmmaker entered his late 30s, another major element of his life changed. In the fall of 1993 Lee lost his status as an eligible bachelor when he wed a lawyer named Tonya Linette Lewis.

Afterword

CLOSING THOUGHTS ABOUT NEW JACK FILMMAKERS

Throughout this book I have attempted to remain as objective as possible, reporting the facts about each film and filmmaker, as opposed to rumors and conjecture so that the reader can hopefully make his or her own informed judgment. When it came time to write these closing thoughts, I felt compelled to offer my opinion about what the future may hold for African American filmmakers.

THE STAGE HAS BEEN SET

In researching this book I began to find patterns and commonalties emerging among the directors featured herein. The stage has been set for the future, I would argue, by many of the filmmakers who made films in what I call the "New Jack Era" (1986-1992).

It is fitting that this book begins and ends with the work of Spike Lee as he certainly cracked open the door to Hollywood for young filmmakers that were to follow. After the success of his third film in 1989, *Do the Right Thing,* Lee had clearly proven that films by, for, and about African Americans could be profitable. I believe Lee's track record served as the catalyst for many of the Hollywood studios to seek their own in-house African American filmmaker. In essence, every studio wanted to have its own "Spike Lee" type director in an effort to capture a piece of the growing African American audience.

By 1990, the studios rushed African American themed films into production and a year later, 12 were released, thus establishing what many consider to be a modern day renaissance for African American filmmakers.

FILMS FROM THE HOOD

During the renaissance year of 1991 *New Jack City* and *Boyz N the Hood,* two dramas set in what is commonly referred to as the "inner-city," garnered considerable attention both by critics and by the moviegoing public. As both films were so profitable compared to other films by African American directors, Hollywood quickly reasoned that the African American audience would only turn out in numbers for violent street dramas. I find this to be not only a misguided and myopic view, but bigoted as well. Just as white audiences are diverse in their tastes, so too are African Americans.

Like many businesses, the Hollywood studios look to the bottom line when deciding what type of product to put before the consumer. I would argue that there is room for a wide range of stories about the African American experience. If Hollywood truly wants to reach an audience, those films will have to be marketed and distributed with care.

The Hollywood perception that only films from the "hood" could be profitable made it difficult for African American filmmakers to interest the studios in anything other than movies like *New Jack* and *Boyz*. Director Mario Van Peebles had extreme difficulty finding the financing for his follow-up to *New Jack City*. Van Peebles had a script for a multi-ethnic western called *Posse* that he wanted to direct, but Hollywood scoffed at the idea. Some executives, according to Van Peebles, referred to his project as "Old Jack City," arguing that the African American audience would not want to see a western. Van Peebles eventually found the necessary funding from a European distributor.

DOIN' IT FOR THEMSELVES

The other alternative to letting Hollywood decide which films will and will not be made is for African Americans to finance, produce, market and distribute their own movies. What is needed, I would contend, is for wealthy African Americans to step forward and put up the money to form a studio. Perhaps someone like Bill Cosby or Michael Jackson. Oprah Winfrey has made steps in the studio direction with her Harpo productions, but the output is sporadic and primarily for a television audience. Robert Johnson, owner of cable's Black Entertainment Television made a foray into filmmaking in 1993 by announcing that he would produce action films featuring African Americans for his newly formed pay-per-view cable channel. In my opinion, Spike Lee would be the best person to operate a studio. He does so on an indirect basis by serving as the executive producer for other filmmakers.

The day when we see a full fledged African American movie studio is approaching fast as a new generation of producers is emerging from the crop of New Jack filmmakers. Among the more prominent are the Hudlin brothers, Jackson and McHenry and actor/producer Damon Wayans. Damon, unlike his brother Keenan, opted to enter the filmmaking arena not as a director, but as a producer of the films he starred in. Using his rising clout as an actor of such films as *The Last Boy Scout,* Wayans served as executive producer of his 1992 comedy *Mo' Money* and his 1994 superhero parody called *Blankman.*

THE FUTURE OF NEW JACK CINEMA

After the Black Film Renaissance of 1991, I would argue that a number of patterns emerged with regard to the direction that African American directors were headed. Movies dealing with young African American males coming of age in the "hood" were profitable, among them, *Boyz N the Hood* and *Juice.* Therefore, the Hollywood studios were each trying to repeat the success of these films.

Some of the older New Jack directors made efforts during the mid 1990s toward directing movies not exclusively about the African American experience. Director Bill Duke's 1993 film, made for the Disney company, *The Cemetery Club,* featured an all white cast and exemplified the desire of some directors to be seen as individuals who could direct any type of movie. Another example of this type of branching out occurred during 1993. In that year, former actor turned director, Thomas Carter's debut film, *Swing Kids,* about boys coming of age in Nazi Germany, was released by Disney.

We will always have African Americans making films for and about African Americans as long as one can gain access to equipment and financing. However, I sincerely hope that those directors wishing to participate in the Hollywood system, to reach a broad audience, will not be "ghettoized", and restricted to films only about stereotypical African Americans.

THE SISTERS ARE COMING UP!

As I finish this book in 1994, one of the encouraging signs of growth in the industry is the emergence of African American women in Hollywood. Debbie Allen, Leslie Harris, and Darnell Martin each received an opportunity to have a voice on the screen by directing films that would go on to receive wide distribution, *Out of Sync, Just Another Girl on the I.R.T.* and *I Like It Like That,* respectively. I am confident, that in the near future, one will be able to fill an entire book with chapters about African American women making films on a large scale.

MY CLOSING WISH FOR THE READER

There are other would-be African American filmmakers, men and women, waiting in the wings and perhaps reading these pages. It is my prayer that each of you be given a chance to tell your stories and perpetuate your culture accurately to the masses.

Steve Kendall
Arlington, VA
October, 1994

Selected Bibliography

Burnett, Charles. "One on One: Charles Burnett and Charles Lane" American Film (August 1991): 40-43.

Dash, Julie. *Daughters of the Dust: The Making of an African American Woman's Film.* New York: The New Press, 1992.

Diawara, Manthia. *Black American Cinema.* New York: Rutledge, 1993.

Diawara, Manthia (guest ed.). "Black Cinema." Wide Angle, vol. 13, numbers 3 & 4 (July-October 1991) entire issue.

Easton, Nina J. "New Black Films, New Insights." Los Angeles Times (3 May 1991): A1, A22.

Jackson, Elizabeth. "Michael Schultz." Black Film Review, vol. 7, no.1: 4-19.

Jones, Jacquie. "Mario Van Peeples: From Jump Street ." Black Film Review, vol. 6, no. 4: 12-15.

Lee, Spike. *Spike Lee's Gotta Have It: Inside Guerrilla Filmmaking.* New York: Simon & Shuster, 1987.

Lee, Spike and Lisa Jones. *Uplift The Race: The Construction of School Daze.* New York: Simon & Shuster, 1988.

Lee, Spike and Lisa Jones. *Do The Right Thing.* New York: Simon & Shuster, 1989.

Lee, Spike and Lisa Jones. *Mo' Better Blues.* New York: Simon & Shuster, 1990.

Lee, Spike. [essays by] Terry McMillan [et al.]; photographs by David Lee. *Five for Five: The Films of Spike Lee.* New York: Stewart, Tabori & Chang, 1991.

Lee, Spike and Ralph Riley. *By Any Means Necessary: The trails and tribulations of the making of Malcolm X.* New York: Hyperion, 1992.

Marshall, Marilyn. "Robert Townsend: Hollywood 'Shuffling' To The Top." Ebony (July 1987): 54-58.

Meisel, Myron. "Burnett's To Sleep With Anger His Ticket to Indie Mainstream." The Film Journal, (October 1990): 14, 84.

Randolph, Laura B. "Robin Givens and Gregory Hines Combine Their Talents In New Movie A Rage In Harlem." Ebony (January 1991): 128-130.

Tate, Greg. "Close-Up: Spike Lee." American Film (September 1986): 48-49.

Verniere, James. "Doing The Job: Spike Lee talks to James Verniere about 'Malcolm X', white audiences, black Muslims and bad press." Sight and Sound (February 1993): 10-11

Wiley, Ralph. "Great 'X'Pectations" (interview with Spike Lee), Premiere (November 1992): 88-96,128.

AFRICAN AMERICAN WOMEN FILMMAKERS

The following bibliography was provided by my brilliant colleague, Frances Gateward. Professor Gateward is a scholar of film studies whose forthcoming dissertation will focus on works by contemporary African American women filmmakers. Her dissertation will analyze the way these filmmakers address racism and sexism through cinematic discourse.

Black Film Review, vol. 2, no. 3, 1986. (issue on Black Women Filmmakers).

Jackson, Elizabeth. "Barbara McCullough, independent filmmaker: 'Know how to do something different.'" Jump Cut, no.36, (1991): 94-97.

Larkin, Sharon Alile. "Black Women Film-makers Defining Ourselves: Feminism in Our Voice." Female Spectators, Looking at Film and Television. New York: Verso, 1988, 157-173.

Mapp, Edward. "Black Women in Films." The Black Scholar. (March-April 1973): 42-46.

Smith, Valerie. "Reconstituting the Image." Callaloo, vol. 11, no. 4, 1988, p. 709-716.

Stephens, Lenora Clodfelter. "Black Women in Film." The South and Film, Warren French (ed). University Press of S. Mississippi: Jackson 1981: 164-169.

White, Deborah Gray. "Ar'n't I a Woman? Jezebel and Mammy: The Mythology of Female Slavery." New York: Norton, 1985, 29-61.

For a comprehensive listing of African American films on video and laserdisk, I reccomend ordering the *Facets African American* Video Guide, compiled by Patrick Ogle.

Facets Video Toll Free Number
1-800-331-6197

Facets Video
1517 West Fullerton Avenue
Chicago, Illinois 60614

Appendix A

Production Credits

Bebe's Kids

Released by Paramount Pictures, 1992
Rated PG-13, Running time: 74 minutes

THE FILMMAKERS

Executive Producers	Reginald and Warrington Hudlin
Producers	Willard Carroll and Thomas L. Wilhite
Director	Bruce Smith
Writer	Reginald Hudlin
Based on Characters Created by	Robin Harris
Editor	Lynne Southerland
Music	John Barnes
Production Design	Fred Cline

WITH THE VOICES OF:

Faizon Love	as Robin Harris
Vanessa Bell Calloway	as Jamika
Wayne Collins, Jr.	as Leon
Jonell Green	as La Shawn
Marques Houston	as Kahlil
Tone Loc	as Pee Wee
Nell Carter	as Vivian
Rich Little	as President Nixon

Boomerang

Released by Paramount Pictures, 1992
Rated R, Running time: 118 minutes

THE FILMMAKERS

Executive Producer	Mark Lipsky
Producers	Brian Grazer and Warrington Hudlin
Director	Reginald Hudlin
Screenplay	Barry W. Blaustein and David Sheffield
Story	Eddie Murphy
Director of Photography	Woody Omens
Editor	Earl Watson
Music	Marcus Miller
Production Design	Jane Musky

THE CAST

Marcus Graham	Eddie Murphy
Jacqueline	Robin Givens
Angela	Halle Berry
Gerard	David Alan Grier
Tyler	Martin Lawrence
Strangé	Grace Jones
Nelson	Geoffrey Holder
Lady Eloise	Eartha Kitt
Bony T	Chris Rock
Yvonne	Tisha Campbell
Todd	John Canada Terrell
Mr. Jackson	John Witherspoon
Mrs. Jackson	Bebe Drake-Massey

Boyz N The Hood

Released by Columbia Pictures, 1991

Rated R, Running time: 112 minutes

THE FILMMAKERS

Producer	Steve Nicolaides
Director	John Singleton
Screenplay	John Singleton
Director of Photography	Charles Mills
Editor	Bruce Cannon
Art Director	Bruce Bellamy
Music	Stanley Clarke

THE CAST

Furious Styles	Larry Fishburne
Tre	Cuba Gooding, Jr.
Dough Boy	Ice Cube
Ricky	Morris Chestnut
Brandi	Nia Long
Reva Styles	Angela Bassett
Mrs. Baker	Tyra Ferrell

Daughters of the Dust

Released by Kino International, 1992

No Rating, Running time: 113 minutes

THE FILMMAKERS

Producer	Julie Dash
Director and Writer	Julie Dash
Director of Photography	Arthur Jafa
Editor	Amy Carey and Joseph Burton
Music	John Barnes
Production Design	Kerry Marshall

THE CAST

Nana Peazant	Cora Lee Day
Haagar Peazant	Kaycee Moore
Eula Peazant	Alva Rogers
Eli Peazant	Adisa Anderson
Yellow Mary	Barbara-O
Viola	Cherly Lynn Bruce

Deep Cover

Released by New Line Cinema, 1991
Rated R, Running time: 107 minutes

THE FILMMAKERS

Executive Producers	Michael De Luca and David Streit
Producers	Pierre David and Henry Bean
Co-Producers	Deborah Moore
Director	Bill Duke
Screenplay	Michael Tolkin and Henry Bean
Story	Michael Tolkin
Director of Photography	Bojan Bazelli
Editor	John Carter
Production Design	Pam Warner
Music	Michel Colombier

THE CAST

Russell Stevens, Jr.	Larry Fishburne
David Jason	Jeff Goldblum
Betty McCutcheon	Victoria Dillard
Carver	Charles Martin Smith
Gopher	Sydney Lassick
Taft	Clarence Willimas III

Def by Temptation

Released by Troma, 1990

Rated R, Running time: 95 minutes

THE FILMMAKERS

Executive Producers	Charles Huggins, Kevin Harewood, and Nelson George
Co-Producers	Kerwin Simms and Hanja O. Moss
Writer, Producer, and Director	James Bond III
Cinematographer	Ernest Dickerson
Editor	Li-Shin Yu
Music Score	Paul Laurence
Production Design	David Carrington
Special Make-up and Visual Effects Creator	Rob Benevides

THE CAST

Joel	James Bond III
"K"	Kadeem Hardison
Dougy	Bill Nunn
Minister Garth	Samuel L. Jackson
Grandma	Minnie Gentry
Married Man	Rony Clanton
Jonathan	Steven Van Cleef
Bartender #1	John Canada Terrell
Bartender #2	Guy Davis
Temptress	Cynthia Bond
Himself	Freddie Jackson
Himself	Najee
Madam Sonya	Melba Moore

Do The Right Thing

Released by Universal, 1989

Rated R, Running time: 2 hours

THE FILMMAKERS

Producer, Writer & Director	Spike Lee
Co-Producer	Monty Ross
Line Producer	John Kilik
Cinematographer	Ernest Dickerson
Editor	Barry Alexander Brown
Original Music Score	Bill Lee
Production Design	Wynn Thomas
Casting	Robi Reed
Costumes	Ruth Carter
Sound Design	Skip Lievsay

THE CAST

Sal	Danny Aiello
Da Mayor	Ossie Davis
Mother Sister	Ruby Dee
Vito	Richard Edson
Buggin' Out	Giancarlo Esposito
Mookie	Spike Lee
Radio Raheem	Bill Nunn
Pino	John Turturro
ML	Paul Benjamin
Coconut Sid	Frankie Faison
Sweet Dick Willie	Robin Harris
Jade	Joie Lee
Clifton	John Savage
Mister Señor Love Daddy	Samuel Jackson
Smiley	Roger Smith
Tina	Rosie Perez

The Five Heartbeats

Released by 20th Century Fox, 1991

Rated R, Running time: 121 minutes

THE FILMMAKERS

Producer	Loretha C. Jones
Director	Robert Townsend
Writer	Robert Townsend and Keenan Ivory Wayans
Director of Photography	Bill Dill
Editor	John Carter
Music	Stanley Clarke
Production Design	Wynn Thomas

THE CAST

Duck	Robert Townsend
Eddie	Michael Wright
J. T.	Leon
Dresser	Harry J. Lennix
Choirboy	Tico Wells
Eleanor Potter	Diahann Carroll
Sarge	Harold Nicholas
Duck's baby sister	Tressa Thomas
Jimmy Potter	Chuck Patterson
Big Red	Hawthorne James

Hangin' With the Homeboys

Released by New Line Cinema, 1991

Rated R, Running time: 89 minutes

THE FILMMAKERS

Producer	Richard Brick
Director and Writer	Joseph B. Vasquez
Director of Photography	Anghel Decca
Editor	Michael Schweitzer

THE CAST

Willie	Doug E. Doug
Tom	Mario Joyner
Johnny	John Leguizamo
Vinny	Nestor Serrano
Vanessa	Kimberly Russell
Luna	Mary B. Ward
Rasta	Reggie Montgomery

Hollywood Shuffle

Released by The Samuel Goldwyn Co.,
1987 Rated R, Running time: 81 minutes

THE FILMMAKERS

Executive Producer	Carl Craig
Producer	Robert Townsend
Associate Producer	Richard Cummings, Jr.
Director	Robert Townsend
Writers	Robert Townsend and Keenan Ivory Wayans
Director of Photography	Peter Deming
Editor	W. D. Garrett
Music	Patrice Rushen and Udi Harpaz
Art Direction	Melba Katzman Farquhar

THE CAST

Bobby Taylor	Robert Townsend
Lydia	Anne-Marie Johnson
Stevie Taylor	Craigus R. Johnson
Bobby's Grandmother	Helen Martin
Bobby's Mother	Starletta DuPois
Donald	Keenan Ivory Wayans
Tiny	Ludie Washington
Mr. Jones	John Witherspoon

House Party

Released by New Line Cinema, 1990

Rated R, Running time: 90 minutes

THE FILMMAKERS

Executive Producer	Gerald T. Olson
Producer	Warrington Hudlin
Writer/Director	Reginald Hudlin
Cinematographer	Peter Deming
Editor	Earl Watson
Music Composers	Marcus Miller and Lenny White
Production Design	Bryan Jones
Casting	Eileen Knight
Costume Designer	Harold Evans

THE CAST

Kid	Christopher Reid
Pop	Robin Harris
Play	Christopher Martin
Bilal	Martin Lawrence
Sidney	Tisha Campbell
Sharane	A. J. Johnson
Stab	Paul Anthony
Pee-Wee	Bowlegged Lou
Killa	B-Fine

House Party 2

Released by New Line Cinema, 1991

Rated R, Running time: 94 minutes

THE FILMMAKERS

Director and Producer	Doug McHenry and George Jackson
Writer	Rusty Cundieff and Daryl G. Nickens
Based on Characters Created by	Reginald Hudlin
Director of Photography	Francis Kenny
Editor	Joel Goodman
Music	Vassal Benford
Production Design	Michelle Minch

THE CAST

Professor Sinclair	Georg Stanford Brown
Mr. Lee	Tony Burton
Sidney	Tisha Campbell
Shelia	Iman
Jamal	Kamron
Zora	Queen Latifah
Kid	Christopher Reid
Play	Christopher Martin
Dean Kramer	William Schallert

I'm Gonna Git You Sucka

Released by United Artists, 1988

Rated R, Running time: 89 minutes

THE FILMMAKERS

Executive Producers	Raymond Katz and Eric L. Gold
Co-Producers	Eric Barrett and Tamara Rawitt
Producers	Peter McCarthy and Carl Craig
Writer/Director	Keenan Ivory Wayans
Director of Photography	Tom Richmond
Editor	Michael R. Miller
Musical Score	David Michael Frank
Casting	Jaki Brown and Robi Reed
Costume Designer	Ruth E. Carter

THE CAST

Jack Spade	Keenan Ivory Wayans
John Slade	Bernie Casey
Flyguy	Antonio Fargas
Kung Fu Joe	Steve James
Hammer	Isaac Hayes
Slammer	Jim Brown
Ma Bell	Ja'net DuBois
Cheryl	Dawnn Lewis
Mr. Big	John Vernon
Willie	Kadeem Hardison
Leonard	Damon Wayans

Juice

Released by Paramount Pictures, 1992
Rated R, Running time: 95 minutes

THE FILMMAKERS

Producers	David Heyman, Neal H. Moritz and Peter Frankfurt
Co-Producer	Preston Holmes
Director	Ernest R. Dickerson
Screenplay	Gerard Brown and Ernest R. Dickerson
Story	Ernest R. Dickerson
Director of Photography	Larry Banks
Editor	Sam Pollard and Brunilda Torres
Production Design	Lester Cohen
Original Score	Hank Shocklee and the Bomb Squad

THE CAST

Q	Omar Epps
Raheem	Khalil Kain
Steel	Jermaine Hopkins
Bishop	Tupac Shakur
Yolanda	Cindy Herron

Jungle Fever

Released by Universal Pictures, 1991
Rated R, Running time: 130 minutes

THE FILMMAKERS

Director, Writer and Producer	Spike Lee
Co-Producer	Monty Ross
Cinematographer	Ernest Dickerson
Editor	Sam Pollard
Music	Stevie Wonder and Terence Blanchard
Production Design	Wynn Thomas

THE CAST

Flipper Purify	Wesley Snipes
Angie Tucci	Annabella Sciorra
Cyrus	Spike Lee
Good Reverend Dr. Purify	Ossie Davis
Lucinda Purify	Ruby Dee
Gator Purify	Samuel L. Jackson
Drew	Lonette McKee
Paulie Carbone	John Turturro
Mike Tucci	Frank Vincent
Lou Carbone	Anthony Quinn
Vivian	Halle Berry
Orin Goode	Tyra Ferrell
Vera	Veronica Webb
Charlie Tucci	David Dundara
James Tucci	Michael Imperioli
Jerry	Tim Robbins
Leslie	Brad Dourif

Livin' Large

Released by The Samuel Goldwyn Company, 1991

Rated R, Running time: 96 minutes

THE FILMMAKERS

Producer	David V. Picker
Director	Michael Schultz
Writer	William M. Payne
Director of Photography	Peter Collister
Editor	Christopher Holmes

THE CAST

Dexter Jackson	T. C. Carson
Toynelle Davis	Lisa Arrindell
Kate Penndragin	Blanche Baker
Baker Moon	Nathaniel Hall
Missy Carnes	Julia Campbell

Malcolm X

Distributed by Warner Bros.,1992

Rated PG-13, Running time: 3 hours, 20 minutes

THE FILMMAKERS

Producers	Marvin Worth and Spike Lee
Co-Producer	Monty Ross, Jon Kilik, and Preston Holmes
Director	Spike Lee
Screenplay	Arnold Perl and Spike Lee Based on the book *The Autobiography of Malcolm X as told to Alex Haley*
Photographer	Ernest Dickerson
Editor	Barry Alexander Brown
Production Design	Wynn Thomas
Original Music Score	Terrence Blanchard

THE CAST

Malcolm X	Denzel Washington
Betty Shabazz	Anglea Bassett
Elijah Muhammad	Al Freeman, Jr.
West Indian Archie	Delroy Lindo
Shorty	Spike Lee

Mo' Better Blues

Released by Universal, 1990

Rated R, Running Time: 129 minutes

THE FILMMAKERS

Producer, Writer and Director	Spike Lee
Co-Producer	Monty Ross
Line Producer	John Kilik
Cinematographer	Ernest Dickerson
Original Music Score	Bill Lee
Editor	Sam Pollard
Sound Design	Skip Lievsay
Production Design	Wynn Thomas
Casting	Robi Reed
Costumes	Ruth E. Carter

THE CAST

Bleek Gilliam	Denzel Washington
Giant	Spike Lee
Shadow Henderson	Wesley Snipes
Left Hand Lacey	Giancarlo Esposito
Butterbean Jones	Robin Harris
Indigo Downes	Joie Lee
Bottom Hammer	Bill Nunn
Moe Flatbush	John Turturro
Big Stop Gilliam	Dick Anthony Williams
Clarke Bentacourt	Cynda Williams

New Jack City

Released by Warner Bros., 1991
Rated R, Running time: 100 minutes

THE FILMMAKERS

Producer	Doug McHenry and George Jackson
Director	Mario Van Peebles
Screenplay	Thomas Lee Wright and Barry Michael Cooper
Story	Thomas Lee Wright
Director of Photography	Francis Kenny
Editor	Steven Kemper
Music	Michel Colombier
Production Design	Charles C. Bennett

THE CAST

Nino Brown	Wesley Snipes
Scotty Appleton	Ice-T
Pookie	Chris Rock
Nick Peretti	Judd Nelson
Detective Stone	Mario Van Peebles
Gee Money	Allen Payne
Keisha	Vanessa Williams
Kim Park	Russell Wong
Duh Duh Duh	Bill Nunn
Gangster	Anthony DeSando

One False Move

Distributed by IRS Releasing, 1992
Rated R, Running time: 105 minutes

THE FILMMAKERS

Executive Producers	Miles A. Copeland, Paul Colichman and Harold Welb
Producers	Jesse Beaton and Ben Myron
Directer	Carl Franklin
Screenplay	Billy Bob Thornton and Tom Epperson
Director of Photography	James L. Carter
Editor	Carole Kravetz
Music	Peter Haycock and Derek Holt

THE CAST

Dale (Hurricane) Dixon	Bill Paxton
Fantasia (Lila)	Cynda Williams
Ray Malcolm	Billy Bob Thornton
Pluto	Michael Beach

Passenger 57

Released by Warner Bros., 1992
Rated R, Running time: 90 minutes

THE FILMMAKERS

Executive Producer	Jonathan Sheinberg
Producers	Lee Rich, Dan Paulson and Dylan Sellers
Co-Producer	Robert J. Anderson
Director	Kevin Hooks
Screenplay	David Loughery and Dan Gordon
Story	Stewart Raffill and Dan Gordon
Director of Photography	Mark Irwin
Editor	Richard Nord
Music	Stanley Clarke

THE CAST

John Cutter	Wesley Snipes
Charles Rane	Bruce Payne
Sly Delvecchio	Tom Sizemore
Marti Slayton	Alex Datcher
Stuart Ramsey	Bruce Greenwood
Dwight Henderson	Robert Hooks
Lisa Cutter	Elena Ayala

A Rage in Harlem

Released by Miramax Films, 1991

Rated R, Running time: 115

THE FILMMAKERS

Producer	Stephen Woolley and Kerry Boyle
Director	Bill Duke
Screenplay	John Toles-Bey and Bobby Crawford
Based on the novel by	Chester Himes
Director of Photography	Toyomichi Kurita
Editor	Curtiss Clayton
Music	Elmer Bernstein
Production Design	Steven Legler

THE CAST

Jackson	Forest Whitaker
Goldy	Gregory Hines
Imabelle	Robin Givens
Big Kathy	Zakes Mokae
Easy Money	Danny Glover
Slim	Badja Djola
Screamin' Jay Hawkins	Himself
Jodie	John Toles-Bey

School Daze

Released by Columbia Pictures, 1988

Rated R, Running time: 114 minutes

THE FILMMAKERS

Executive Producer	Grace Blake
Co-Producers	Monty Ross and Loretha C. Jones
Producer, Writer & Director	Spike Lee
Cinematographer	Ernest Dickerson
Editor	Barry Alexander Brown
Sound Design	Maurice Schell
Production Design	Wynn Thomas
Casting	Robi Reed
Choreography	Otis Sallid
Costumes	Ruthe Carter

THE CAST

Dap Dunlap	Larry Fishburne
Julian "Big Brother Almighty"	Giancarlo Esposito
Jane Toussaint	Tisha Campbell
Rachel Meadows	Kyme
Half-Pint	Spike Lee
Coach Odom	Ossie Davis
President McPherson	Joe Seneca

She's Gotta Have It

Released by Island Pictures, 1986
Rated R, Running time: 100 minutes

THE FILMMAKERS

Producer	Shelton J. Lee
Associate Producer	Pamm Jackson
Writer, Director & Editor	Spike Lee
Cinematographer	Ernest Dickerson
Music	Bill Lee
Production Supervisor	Monty Ross
Production Design	Wynn Thomas
Sound Design	Barry Brown

THE CAST

Nola Darling	Tracy Camilla Johns
Jamie Overstreet	Tommy Hicks
Mars Blackmon	Spike Lee
Geer Childs	John Canada Terrell
Clorinda Bradford	Joie Lee
Opal Gilstrap	Raye Dowell
Sonny Darling	Bill Lee
Dr. Jamison	Epatha Mekerson

Straight Out of Brooklyn

Released by The Samuel Goldwyn Co., 1991
Rated R, Running time: 91 minutes

THE FILMMAKERS

Executive Producers	Lindsay Law and Ira Deutchman
Producer	Matty Rich
Associate Producer	Allen Black
Director	Matty Rich
Screenplay	Matty Rich
Editor	Jack Haigis
Director of Photography	John Rosnell
Original Score Composed	Harold Wheeler

THE CAST

Ray Brown	George T. Odom
Frankie Brown	Ann D. Sanders
Dennis Brown	Lawrence Gilliard, Jr.
Carolyn Brown	Barbara Sanon
Shirley	Reana E. Drummond
Larry	Matty Rich
Kevin	Mark Malone
Luther	Ali Shahid Abdul Wahha
Saledene	Joseph A. Thomas
James	James McFadden
Ms. Walker	Dorise Black

Strictly Business

Released by Warner Bros., 1991

Rated PG-13, Running time: 83 minutes

THE FILMMAKERS

Producer	Andre Harrelland Pam Gibson
Director	Kevin Hooks
Writer	Pam Gibson and Nelson George
Director of Photography	Zoltan David
Editor	Richard Nord
Music	Michel Colombier
Production Design	Ruth Ammon

THE CAST

Bobby	Tommy Davidson
Waymon	Joseph C. Phillips
Natalie	Halle Berry
Diedre	Anne Marie Johnson
David	David Marshall Grant
Drake	Jon Cypher
Monroe	Sam Jackson
Millicent	Kim Coles
Leroy Halloran	James McDaniel
Larry	Paul Provenza
Sheila	Annie Golden
Gary	Sam Rockwell
Mr. Atwell	Ira Wheeler

Talkin' Dirty After Dark

Released by New Line Cinema, 1991

Rated R, Running time: 86 minutes

THE FILMMAKERS

Executive Producer	Kevin Moreton
Producer	Patricia A. Stallone
Director and Writer	Topper Carew
Director of Photography	Misha Suslov
Editor	Claudia Finkle
Production Design	Naomi Shohan

THE CAST

Terry	Martin Lawrence
Dookie	John Witherspoon
Aretha	Phyllis Yvonne Stickney
Ruby Lin	Jedda Jones
Percy	Darryl Sivan
Mark Curry	Antonio
Bigg	"Tiny" Lister, Jr.

To Sleep With Anger

Released by The Samuel Goldwyn Co., 1990
Rated PG, Running Time: 110 minutes

THE FILMMAKERS

Executive Producers	Edward R. Pressman, Danny Glover, and Harris E. Tulchin
Producers	Caledcot Chubb, Thomas S. Brynes and Darin Scott
Associate Producers	Michael Flynn and Linda Koulisis
Writer and Director	Charles Burnett
Director of Photographer	Walt Lloyd
Editor	Nancy Richardson
Production Design	Penny Barrett
Music Composer	Stephen James Taylor

THE CAST

Harry	Danny Glover
Gideon	Paul Butler
Suzie	Mary Alice
Junior	Carl Lumbly
Pat	Vonetta McGee
Babe Brother	Richard Brooks
Linda	Sheryl Lee Ralph
Hattie	Ethel Ayler

True Identity

Released by Touchstone Pictures, 1991

Rated R, Running time: 92 minutes

THE FILMMAKERS

Producers	Carol Baum and Teri Schwartz
Director	Charles Lane
Writer	Andy Breckman
Director of Photography	Tom Ackerman
Editor	Kent Beyda
Music	Marc Marder
Production design	John DeCuir, Jr.

THE CAST

Miles	Lenny Henry
Carver	Frank Langella
Duane	Charles Lane
Houston	J. T. Walsh
Kristi	Anne-Marie Johnson
Anthony	Andreas Katsulas
Harvey Cooper	Michael McKean

Appendix B

Filmography of Directors from the New Jack Era

James Bond III
Def by Temptation (1990)

Debbie Allen
Out of Sync (in production, 1994, for BET films)

Charles Burnett
To Sleep With Anger (1990)
The Glass Shield (in production, 1994)

Topper Carew
Talkin' Dirty After Dark (1991)

Thomas Carter
Swing Kids (1993)

Julie Dash
Daughters of the Dust (1991)

Ernest Dickerson
Juice (1991)
Rules of the Game (1994)

Bill Duke
A Rage in Harlem (1991)
Deep Cover (1992)
Cemetery Club (1993)
Sister Act 2: Back in the Habit (1994)

Carl Franklin
One False Move (1992)
Devil in a Blue Dress (in production, 1994)

Morgan Freeman
Bopha! (1993)

Leslie Harris
Just Another Girl on the I.R.T. (1993)
First African American women to have a film released by a major distributor, Miramax.

Allen and Albert Hughes (Twin brothers)
Menace II Society (1993)

Kevin Hooks
Strictly Business (1991)
Passenger 57 (1992)

The Hudlin Brothers (Reginald and Warrington)
House Party! (1990)
Boomerang (1992)
BeBe's Kids (1992), screenwriter and producer, respectively

David Johnson
Drop Squad (1994)
Spike Lee served as executive producer

Charles Lane
True Identity (1991)

Spike Lee
She's Gotta Have It (1986)
School Daze (1988)
Do the Right Thing (1989)
Mo' Better Blues (1990)
Jungle Fever (1991)
Malcolm X (1992)
Crooklyn (1994)
Clockers (in production, 1994)

McHenry & Jackson (Doug and George, respectively)
House Party 2 (1992)
House Party 3 (1993), producers

Doug McHenry
Jason's Lyric (1994)

Matty Rich
Straight Out of Brooklyn (1991)
The Inkwell (1994)

Michael Schultz
Livin' Large (1991)

John Singleton
Boyz N The Hood (1991)
Poetic Justice (1993)
Higher Learning (1995)

Robert Townsend
Hollywood Shuffle (1987)
The Five Heartbeats (1991)
The Meteor Man (1994)

Mario Van Peebles
New Jack City (1991)
Posse (1993)
Panther (1995)

Darnell Martin
I Like It Like That (1994)
The first African American woman to direct a movie produced by a major Hollywood studio, Columbia Pictures.

Vasquez Joseph
Hangin' with the Homeboys (1991)

Damon Wayans (Executive Producer)
Mo' Money (1992)
Blankman (1994)

Keenan Ivory Wayans
I'm Gonna Git You Sucka (1988)
Low Down Dirty Shame (1994)

Appendix C

Box Office Figures

The following films are listed according to their domestic (United States and Canadian) theatrical rentals. The rental figures consist of the dollar amount collected by the distributor after the theater owners deduct their share. The distributor usually receives the largest percentage of the box office gross during the first two weeks of a film's release. The source for all figures is *Variety* magazine.

NEW JACK DIRECTORS-TOP BOX OFFICE FILMS OF 1993:

Film title	Domestic film rentals (in millions of dollars)
Sister Act 2	35.6
Menace II Society	27.9
Poetic Justice	27.5
Posse	18.3
The Meteor Man	8.0
The Cemetery Club	6.0
Malcolm X (1993 gross, 1992 release)	5.8
Swing Kids	5.6
Passenger 57 (1993 gross, 1992 release)	3.4
Just Another Girl on the I.R.T.	.4
Bopha!	.2

Menace II Society, according to *Variety* magazine, had the best cost to return ratio, of all films directed by an African American in 1993. The film was made with a budget of $3.5 million and grossed $27.7 million at the box office, which amounts to a cost to return ratio of 92.3.

NEW JACK DIRECTORS-TOP BOX OFFICE FILMS OF 1992:

Film title	Domestic film rentals (in millions of dollars)
Boomerang	34.0
Malcolm X	25.0
Mo' Money	19.2
Passenger 57	18.0
Juice	9.2
Deep Cover	7.2
BeBe's Kids	4.0

Juice was one of the most profitable films by an African American in 1992 with an approximate 36% return on its initial cost of $11 million (distribution and marketing costs included with the film's budget).

NEW JACK DIRECTORS-TOP BOX OFFICE FILMS FOR 1991:

Film title	Domestic film rentals (in millions of dollars)
Boyz N the Hood	26.7
New Jack City	22.0
Jungle Fever	15.6
House Party 2	9.5
A Rage in Harlem	4.2

SELECTED LIST OF ALL-TIME TOP BOX OFFICE FILMS BY AFRICAN AMERICANS (1971 – FEBRUARY 1994):

Film title	Domestic film rentals (in millions of dollars)
Stir Crazy (Sidney Poitier, 1980)	58.4
Boomerang	34.0
Harlem Nights (Eddie Murphy, 1989)	33.0
Purple Rain (Prince 1984)	31.7

Boyz N the Hood	26.7
Eddie Murphy Raw	24.8
New Jack City	22.0
Sister Act 2	21.3
Malcolm X	19.4
Mo' Money	19.2
Bustin' Loose (Oz Scott, 1981)	15.4
Let's Do It Again (Sidney Poitier, 1975)	11.8
The Last Dragon (Michael Schultz, 1985)	11.5
Sgt. Pepper's Lonelyhearts Club Band (Michael Schultz, 1978)	11.4
Ghost Dad (Sidney Poitier, 1990)	11.3
Which Way Is Up? (Michael Schultz, 1977)	8.7
Car Wash (Michael Schultz, 1976)	8.5
Jo Jo Dancer Your Life Is Calling (Richard Pryor, 1986)	8.0
Greased Lightning (Michael Schultz, 1977)	7.6
Beat Street (Stan Lathan, 1976)	7.6
Uptown Saturday Night (Sidney Poitier, 1974)	7.4
Richard Pryor — Here and Now (Richard Pryor, 1983)	7.2
Shaft (Gordon Parks, 1971)	7.1
Mahogany (Berry Gordy, 1971)	6.9
A Piece of the Action (Sidney Poitier, 1977)	6.7
Superfly (Gordon Parks, Jr., 1972)	6.4
Under the Cherry Moon (Prince, 1986)	5.8
Cotton Comes to Harlem (Ossie Davis, 1970)	5.1
Hanky Panky (Sidney Poitier, 1982)	5.1
Krush Groove (Michael Schultz, 1985)	5.1
Disorderlies (Michael Schultz, 1987)	4.4
Carbon Copy (Michael Schultz, 1981)	4.2

Sweet Sweet Back's Baadaassss Song (Melvin Van Peeples, 1970)	4.1
Penitentiary (Jamaa Fanaka, 1980)	4.0
Scavenger Hunt (Michael Schultz, 1979)	3.8
Shaft's Big Score (Gordon Parks, 1974)	3.7
Three the Hard Way (Gordon Parks, Jr., 1974)	3.5

MISCELLANEOUS STUFF ABOUT AFRICAN AMERICANS AND MOVIES:

•African Americans make up 25% of the moviegoing audience.

•In 1984, the average number of days African American actors worked in Hollywood was 7. By 1990, that average decreased to 4 days.

•The percentage of the Screen Actors Guild that is African American is approximately 8.

•Minority writers make 63 cents for every dollar earned by a white writer.

•The percentage of African American writers in the Writers Guild is 1.5.

•In 1991, there where more films directed by African Americans, released in theaters, than in the entire previous decade combined.

Sources: Blacks in American Films and Television; NAACP; Black Filmmakers Foundation.

Appendix D

Selected List of Screenwriting Contests

America's Best
c/o The Writer's Foundation, Inc.
1801 Burnet Avenue
Syracuse, NY 13206

Chesterfield Film Company Writer's Film Project
100 Universal Plaza, Bldg. 131
Universal City, CA 91608
(818) 777-3425

Christopher Columbus
Screenplay Discovery Awards
433 N. Camden, Suite 600
Beverly Hills, CA 90210

Hanover Square Productions
7612 Fountain Avenue
Los Angeles, CA 90046
(213) 851-6187

Houston International Film Festival
P.O. Box 56566
Houston, TX 77256
(713) 965-9955

Kentucky Film Arts Coalition Contest
Kentucky Film Arts Coalition
Screenwriting Contest
P.O. Box 679
Lexington, KY 40586-0679

Lee Rich Screenwriting Competition
William Miller, Coordinator
School of Telecommunications
Ohio University
Athens, OH 45701-2979

Malcom Vincent Screenwriting Competition
279 South Beverly Drive
Suite 17
Beverly Hills, CA 90212

Minority Writers Trainee Program
Twentieth Television
New Writer's Program 88/262
P.O. Box 900
Beverly Hills, CA 90213

Nicholl Fellowships in Screenwriting
Academic of Motion Picture Arts and Sciences
8949 Wilshire Blvd.
Beverly Hills, CA 90211-1972
(213) 278-8990

Southern Screenwriting Competition
Image Film/Video Center
75 Bennett Street NW, Suite M-1
Atlanta, GA 30309
(404) 352-4225

Southwest Writers Workshop Contest
P.O. Box 14636
Albuquerque, NM 87111
(505) 293-0303

Sundance Institute
4000 Warner Blvd.
Burbank, CA 91522
(818) 954-4776

Television Series Writing Competition
School of Telecommunications
Ohio University
Athens, OH 45701-2979

Virginia Governor's Screenwriting Competition
The Virginia Film Office
P.O. Box 798
Richmond, VA 23206-0789
(804) 371-8204

Walt Disney Pictures Screenwriter's Fellowship
500 South Buena Vista Street
Burbank, CA 91521
(818) 560-6994

Wisconsin Screenwriters Forum
c/o Peggy Williams
221 Frigate Drive
Madison, WI 53705

Writer's Guild of America, East
555 West 57th Street, Suite 1230
New York, NY 10019
(212) 245-6180

Writers Digest
Writing Contest
1507 Dana Avenue
Cincinnati, OH 45207

For additional contest information, you may want to subscribe to:
Hollywood Scriptwriter
1626 N. Wilcox, #385
Hollywood, CA 90028

Freelance Screenwriter's Forum
Box 7
Baldwin, MD 21013

Appendix E

Selected List of Film and Video Festivals

DOMESTIC FESTIVALS:

AFI East-Los Angeles
2021 North Western Ave.
P.O. Box 27999
Los Angeles, CA 90027
(213) 856-7600

AFI National Video Festival
2021 North Western Ave.
Los Angeles, CA 90027
(213) 856-7600

American Children's Television Festival/Ollie Awards
1400 East Touhy
Des Plaines, IL 60018
(706) 390-8700

Asian American International Film Festival
Asian CineVision
35 E. Broadway, 4th Floor
New York, NY 10002
(212) 925-8685

Asian American International Video Festival
Asian CineVision
35 E. Broadway, 4th Floor
New York, NY 10002
(212) 925-8685

Asian Pacific American International Film and Video Festival
Visual Communications
263 So. Los Angeles Street, #307
Los Angeles, CA 90012
(213) 680-4462

Aspen Shorts Festival
P.O. Box 8910
601 E. Bleeker
Aspen, CO. 81612
(303) 925-6882

Baltimore African-American Film Festival
Baltimore Film Forum
Baltimore Museum of Art
10 Art Museum Drive
Baltimore, MD 21218
(410) 889-1993

Big Muddy Film Festival
Dept. of Cinema and Photography
Southern Illinois University
Carbondale, IL. 62904
(618) 453-1475

Black American Cinema Society Film Festival/Independent Filmmakers Awards
Western States Black Research Center
3617 Montclair Street
Los Angeles, CA 90018
(213) 737-3585

Black Filmmakers Hall of Fame Black Independent Film, Video and Screenplay Competition
405 14th Street, Suite 515
Oakland, CA 94612
(510) 465-0804

Blacklight: A Festival of Black International Cinema
Film Center of the School of the Art Institute of Chicago
Columbus Drive at Jackson
Chicago, IL. 60603
(312) 443-3733

CEBA Awards
World Institute of Black Communications, Inc.
463 Seventh Ave.
New York, NY 10019
(212) 714-1508

Chicago Latino Film Festival
Columbia College
600 S. Michigan Ave.
Chicago, IL. 60605
(312) 431-1330

CINE-Council on Non-Theatrical Events
1001 Connecticut Ave., NW
Washington, DC 20036
(202) 785-1136

College Film Festival
University of Cincinnati Film Society
Mail Location 136
Cincinnati, OH 45221
(513) 556-3456

Dance on Camera Festival
Dance Films Association
1133 Broadway, Room 507
New York, NY 10010
(212) 727-0754

International Festival of Films by Women Directors
Seattle, Washington
(206) 621-2231

International Film and TV Festival of New York/
The New York Festivals
655 Avenue of the Americas, 2nd Floor
New York, NY 10010
(914) 238-4481

New Directors/New Films
(212) 875-5610

Rochester Association of Black Communicators Black Film Festival
Killingsworth Communications and Associates
184 Dorchester Rd.
Rochester, NY 14610-1327
(716) 288-5607

San Antonio Cine Festival
1300 Guadalupe Street
San Antonio, TX 78201
(512) 271-3151

San Jose State Student Film and Video Festival
Associated Students Program Board
San Jose State University
Student Union Rm. 350
San Jose, CA 95192
(408) 924-6260

Student Academy Awards
Academy of Motion Picture Arts and Sciences
8949 Wilshire Blvd.
Beverly Hills, CA 90211-1972
(310) 247-3000

Sundance Film Festival
3619 Motor Avenue, Suite 240
Los Angeles, CA 90034
(310) 204-2091

United States Student Film and Video Festival
Film Front
206 Performing Arts Bldg.
University of Utah
Salt Lake City, UT 84112
(801) 328-3646

Visions of U.S.
Video Contest
P.O. Box 200
Hollywood, CA 90078
(213) 856-7745

Washington D.C. International Film Festival/Filmfest
P.O. Box 21396
Washington, D.C. 20009
(202) 727-2396

Women in Film Festival
6464 Sunset Blvd., Suite 660
Los Angeles, California 90028
(213) 463-6050

Women in the Director's Chair Film and Video Festival
3435 N. Sheffield Ave., #3
Chicago, IL 60657
(312) 281-4988

INTERNATIONAL FESTIVALS AND TELEPHONE NUMBERS:

Berlin International Film Festival & European Film Market
Berlin, Germany
4930-254-890

Brussels Festival of Cartoon & Animated Films
Brussells, Belgium
322-477-1555

Cannes International FilmFest
Paris, France
1 42 66 9220

Cartagena International Festival
Cartagena, Colombia
753-642-345

Dublin Film Festival
Dublin, Ireland
353-1-679-2937

Fantastic Film Festival
Brussells, Belgium
322-242-1713

Hong Kong International Film Festival
Hong Kong
852-734-2900

International Animation Festival
Cardiff, UK
44-71-580-6202

Monte Carlo International TV Festival
3393-304-227

Singapore International Film Festival
Singapore
65-738-7567

Tampere International Film Festival
Tampere, Finland
358-31-213-0034

For a comprehensive listing of film and video festivals, I highly recommend the *Association of Independent Video and Filmmakers' (AIVF) Guide to International Film and Video Festivals* by Kathryn Bowser: AIVF, 625 Broadway, 9th Floor, New York, NY 10012

Appendix F

Selected List of Professional Organizations for Filmmakers

Association of Independent Video and Filmmakers, Inc.
625 Broadway, 9th Floor
New York, NY 10012

Black Filmmaker Foundation (BFF) - East Coast Office
375 Greenwich Street
Suite 600
New York, NY 10013
(212) 941-3944

Black Filmmaker Foundation (BFF) - West Coast Office
2049 Century Park
42nd Floor
Los Angeles, CA 90067
310/201-9579

Sundance Institute
4000 Warner Blvd.
Burbank, CA 91522
(818) 954-4776

Warner Brothers Television Comedy Writing Workshop
Prof. John Douglass
The American University
4400 Massachusetts Ave., N.W.
Washington, D.C. 20016
(202) 885-2045 Los Angeles hotline: (818) 954-2933

Writer's Guild of America, East
555 West 57th
Suite 1230
New York, NY 10019
(212) 757-4360

Index

C

D

H

I

J

Design: Jane Jeffry/XY&I
Project coordination & production: Maria Yap & Jenny McMahon/Option X

Order Forms

For additional copies of this book please use the form below

Please Send ________ copies
($14.95 each plus $1.75 shipping and handling
to

JL Denser, Inc.
PO Box 9181
Silver Spring, MD, 20916

____

Name

____

Address

____

City, Zip, State

Please Send ________ copies
($14.95 each plus $1.75 shipping and handling
to

JL Denser, Inc.
PO Box 9181
Silver Spring, MD, 20916

____

Name

____

Address

____

City, Zip, State